Alan C McLean

Profile

UK

HEINEMANN

Contents

Introduction

What is the UK?

The UK's full name is the *United Kingdom of Great Britain and Northern Ireland*. Great Britain is made up of England, Wales, and Scotland.

However, the most commonly used name for the whole country is 'Britain' and inhabitants of the UK usually describe themselves as being 'British'.

The country's head of state is Queen Elizabeth II.

The UK is governed by Parliament. There are two Houses of Parliament: the House of Lords (an unelected assembly) and the House of Commons (an elected assembly).

Key dates in the history of the UK

55 BC:	Roman invasion of Britain.
410–924:	Invasions by Saxons, Danes, Jutes, Vikings, etc.
924:	Athelstan, first king of England.
1066:	Normans win Battle of Hastings. William I King of England.
1301:	England and Wales united.
1485–1603:	Royal House of Tudor. Henry VIII excommunicated by Pope. Assumes title 'Defender of the faith'. Elizabeth I (1558–1603). Golden Age of exploration (Drake, Raleigh) and literature (Shakespeare).
1603:	James VI of Scotland becomes King of Scotland and England as James I.
1649:	Charles I executed. Monarchy abolished by Cromwell.
1660:	Charles II restores monarchy.
1707:	Scotland and England united by Act of Union.
1832:	Great Reform Act extends voting rights.
1870:	Education Act establishes government-controlled schools.
1876:	Queen Victoria becomes Empress of India. British Empire in Africa and Asia at its peak.
1914–1918:	First World War.
1919:	Women win the right to vote.
1939–1945:	Second World War.
1940:	Winston Churchill becomes Prime Minister. Battle of Britain.
1945:	Labour government elected. National Health Service set up.
1947:	Independence of India and Pakistan.
1979–1990:	Margaret Thatcher, longest-serving Prime Minister.

Happy and glorious?

Britain has a royal family but what do they do? What about Prince Charles and Princess Diana, should they voice their opinions? What is Britain's Royal Family for?

Section A

1

What do you know about the British monarchy? Can you answer these questions?

1 How long has the present British monarch reigned?
2 How much power does the Royal Family have?

2

Look at the Royal Family Tree below and read the profiles on page 3. Can you match the profiles with the official titles of members of the Royal Family?

How much of the information from the profiles did you already know?

3

Read the profiles again and look at the photographs.

a Which two ceremonies are shown in two of the photographs?
b Which two organisations' work is shown in the other two photographs?

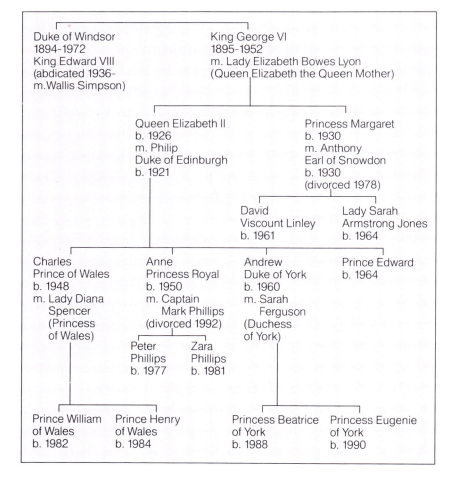

Duke of Windsor
1894–1972
King Edward VIII
(abdicated 1936–
m. Wallis Simpson)

King George VI
1895–1952
m. Lady Elizabeth Bowes Lyon
(Queen Elizabeth the Queen Mother)

Queen Elizabeth II
b. 1926
m. Philip
Duke of Edinburgh
b. 1921

Princess Margaret
b. 1930
m. Anthony
Earl of Snowdon
b. 1930
(divorced 1978)

David
Viscount Linley
b. 1961

Lady Sarah
Armstrong Jones
b. 1964

Charles
Prince of Wales
b. 1948
m. Lady Diana
  Spencer
  (Princess
  of Wales)

Anne
Princess Royal
b. 1950
m. Captain
  Mark Phillips
  (divorced 1992)

Andrew
Duke of York
b. 1960
m. Sarah
  Ferguson
  (Duchess
  of York)

Prince Edward
b. 1964

Peter
Phillips
b. 1977

Zara
Phillips
b. 1981

Prince William
of Wales
b. 1982

Prince Henry
of Wales
b. 1984

Princess Beatrice
of York
b. 1988

Princess Eugenie
of York
b. 1990

4

The notes below (1–6) refer to two more members of the Royal Family.

a Who do they describe?

b Separate the notes and write profiles about the two people. Use any extra information provided in the Family Tree.

1 given title after marriage in 1986

2 married Duke of York, second son of George V, in 1923

3 educated at Gordonstoun School (Scotland), Lakefield College (Canada) and the Royal Naval College, Dartmouth

4 commissioned in the Royal Marines, qualifying as a helicopter pilot and seeing active service in 1982

5 since George VI's death in 1952 has continued to undertake many public duties at home and abroad

6 became Queen in 1937 after abdication of brother-in-law, Edward VIII

5

Work in a group and discuss these questions.

a How much information from this section did you already know?

b Is there anything in the section that surprises you?

c Would you like to be a member of the Royal Family? Do you think it is an easy life?

d Is there a royal family in your country? If not, is there someone who is considered the head of state? What are the advantages and disadvantages of a monarchy and a republic?

Royal Family Profiles

1

_____ became British monarch on 6 February 1952 upon the death of her father, King George VI. She was crowned the following year in Westminster Abbey. Her official birthday, the second Saturday in June, is marked by the Trooping of the Colour, a ceremony during which regiments of the Guards Division and the Household Cavalry parade (troop) the regimental flag (colour) before the sovereign.

She has an income of £7.9 million per year from the civil list (an annual allowance approved by Parliament, made to members of the Royal Family for the expense involved in carrying out their public duties).

Among her many duties are the regular visits she makes to foreign countries, and especially those of the Commonwealth, whose interests and welfare are very important to her.

2

_____ is the Queen's eldest son and heir-apparent to the throne. He was given this title, traditionally given by the British sovereign to his or her eldest son at Caernarfon Castle in Wales, in 1969.

The Prince is well-known as a keen promoter of British causes abroad and of the interests of the general public at home. He set up the Prince's Trust in 1976 to provide recreation and leisure facilities for deprived young people.

3

_____ is the principal title of the Queen's husband. It was bestowed upon him after his marriage to the then Princess Elizabeth in 1947.

The Duke has taken a great deal of interest in the achievements of young people – in 1956 he founded the Duke of Edinburgh's Award Scheme (through which awards are made to young people between the ages of 14 and 21 for enterprise, initiative and achievement).

4

_____ is the Queen's only daughter and eighth in line to the throne. She was given this title by her mother in 1987.

She is a keen and capable horsewoman and won the European Championships in 1971. For this she was voted Sports Personality of the Year by millions of TV viewers. She also represented Britain in the 1976 Olympics in Montreal. Since 1970 she has gained admiration and respect for her tireless work as President of the Save the Children Fund.

Section B

1

Work with a partner.

Look at the front page of the *Daily Mail* opposite. Can you name the people in the photograph? What do you know about them?

2

Read the two news stories from the *Daily Mail* quickly. Answer these questions.

a Where were Prince Charles and Princess Diana 'yesterday'?

b Who were they speaking to?

c What were the themes of their speeches?

3

Read the extracts again. Choose the two sentences from those below which best summarise the main points of the two speeches.

a Prince Charles attacked 'educationists' who promote teaching methods which neglect both students' cultural heritage and their accuracy in the basic skills.

b Prince Charles said in his speech that if teachers use methods that are currently promoted by 'experts' they will be teaching only topics of contemporary interest which are relatively easy for their students to understand.

c Princess Diana described the confused understanding of HIV that exists and encouraged people to overcome their fear of touching people with the virus.

d Princess Diana outlined the tragic situation of children with the HIV virus and the need for people to overcome their negative feelings towards those with the virus.

4

Work in a group of three. Imagine you are each one of the following people:

a a parent

b a teacher

c a member of the audience

Discuss how you would react to the two speeches.

Project

Work in a group to prepare newspaper coverage of a visit by two members of the British Royal Family to your country (or city).

a *Decide which two members of the Royal Family made the visit. Think about the length of their stay and the reasons for their visit.*

b *Decide how many articles and photographs you want to include in the newspaper. Choose aspects of the visit (e.g. a speech, a ceremony, a visit to a home, school or hospital, what they wore) that you would like to cover.*

c *Research information which may be useful when writing the articles. (For example, find out about a real visit by a head of state.)*

d *Write the articles and captions. Choose photographs or draw pictures to accompany them.*

STAND UP TO THE TRENDIES

By RAY MASSEY and GERAINT JONES

PRINCE Charles yesterday accused 'shadowy education experts' of betraying generations of British youngsters.

In an impassioned attack, he said they were robbing children of their rich cultural heritage, particularly Shakespeare.

He savaged progressive teaching methods and 'silly fashions' as unlikely to instil 'fundamental standards of accuracy in the basic skills'.

Parents, he said, should 'call the experts' bluff' and tell them they were talking nonsense.

Conservative politicians warmly welcomed his remarks, while teaching unions and Labour backed his demands for more resources for education and greater help for 'demoralised' staff. Only the National Association for Teachers of English, was critical, dismissing the speech as 'nonsense'.

The speech, to an audience of 350 academics at Stratford's Swan Theatre, marked Shakespeare's birthday, and the Prince was at his most fervent in dealing with the threat to the country's literary heritage. Charles warned that Shakespeare and the classics, which put British people in touch with their roots and spiritual traditions, had all but vanished from some schools.

He said: 'There are terrible dangers in so following fashionable trends in education – trends towards the 'relevant', the exclusively contemporary, the immediately palatable – that we end up with an entire generation of culturally disinherited young people.

'I for one don't want to see that happen. Nor, I suspect, do countless parents up and down the nation, who probably feel utterly powerless in the face of yet another profession, this time the "educationists", which I believe has become increasingly out of touch with the true feelings of so-called ordinary people.'

Charles and Diana en route to Brazil where the Princess will meet Aids patients.

'Give the tragic children a hug'

By SEAN POULTER

PRINCESS Diana pleaded with parents and teachers yesterday not to shun children who have the Aids virus.

She urged people to give the tragic youngsters a hug, adding: 'Heaven knows – they need it.'

Opening a London conference on children and Aids, she spoke movingly of the plight of youngsters who have HIV – the virus which causes the deadly disease – and the need to dispel the prejudice they endure.

The Princess told an audience of health professionals and volunteers: 'HIV does not make people dangerous to know, so you can shake hands and give them a hug.

'What's more, you can share their homes, their workplaces, their playgrounds and their toys.'

Making her first speech as patron of the National Aids Trust, Diana spoke of the 'untold private suffering' behind a confused picture of HIV.

She said it was wrong to dismiss the virus as a problem facing only drug addicts and homosexuals.

Section C

1

a Look back over the unit again and complete the fact file. Research any questions you do not know the answers to.

b Check your answers on page 84.

F*actfile* | **Royal Family**

1
Britain is a constitutional monarchy. The sovereign is head of .... but not head of government. On the advice of the biggest political party in parliament, the sovereign officially appoints the head of government (Prime Minister). Since the time of King George III in the eighteenth century, no monarch has attempted to head the ....

2
Queen Elizabeth II, the current British monarch, was crowned in ....

3
She has four children. Prince Charles, the eldest, is heir to the throne. His elder son, Prince ...., is next in line.

4
Princess Anne married Mark Phillips in 1973, Prince Charles married Lady Diana Spencer in 1981 and Prince .... married Sarah Ferguson in 1986. All three couples have two children. The Queen's youngest son, Prince ...., is unmarried.

5
The Queen was born on 25 April .... She also has an official birthday in the month of .... This is marked by one of many state occasions – the 'Trooping of the Colour'.

6
The Queen receives £7.9 .... a year of taxpayer's money. In return, she carries out many public duties. This includes the Opening of Parliament, receiving heads of state from other countries and travelling extensively overseas.

7
The other members of the Royal Family, including the Queen Mother who is over 90 years old, also carry out many official .... and public duties.

8
The Queen's second son, ..., is a .... pilot in the Royal Navy. He has seen active service.

9
Prince Edward is involved in theatre. Like Prince ...., he studied history at Cambridge University.

10
The Queen Mother remains one of the most popular members of the Royal Family. She became Queen in .... after the abdication of her brother-in-law ....

The voice of the people

Britain is governed by Parliament. How are Members of Parliament elected? What involvement does the Queen have with Parliament? Why aren't there more women in Parliament?

Section A

1

What do you know about the British Parliament? How many of the questions in the factfile can you answer?

2

Work with a partner.
a Discuss your answers.
b Check your answers on page 84.
c Do any of these facts surprise you?

 Factfile | Parliament

1
The first Parliament in Britain was held in . . . ?
a 1066 b 1241 c 1605

2
There are two 'houses' in the British Parliament. One is called the House of Commons. What is the other called?

3
Members of the House of Commons are called Members of Parliament (MPs). How many MPs are there?

a fewer than 500
b fewer than 600
c more than 600

4
Approximately how many of these MPs are women?

a less than 5%
b less than 10%
c less than 20%

5
Each MP represents an area of the country. This area is called . . . .

a a place b a constituency
c a post

6
The head of the British government is called . . . .

a the Prime Minister
b the President
c the Leader

7
Margaret Thatcher was Prime Minister from 1979 to 1990. She was the first woman Prime Minister . . . .

a since 1900
b since 1800
c that Britain had had

8
How old do you have to be to vote in a general election?
a 16 b 18 c 21

9
Governments are elected in general elections, where everyone is entitled to vote. In Britain a general election is held . . . .

a every four years
b every five years
c whenever the government wants, but within five years

10
After every general election, MPs elect one of their number to chair their debates and to make sure they obey the rules of Parliament. This MP is called . . . .

a the Lord Chancellor
b the Speaker
c the Chairman

11
When an MP dies . . . .
a his/her seat remains vacant until the next general election
b another MP takes over the seat
c a local election is held to choose a new MP

12
Which three of the following are the largest British parties?

a Plaid Cymru
b the Communist Party
c the Conservative Party
d the Green Party
e the Labour Party
f the Liberal Democrats
g the National Front
h the Scottish National Party

Section B

1

a Look at the headline of the article and the photograph. Who do you think opens Parliament?

b Now read the first paragraph and check your answer.

c Read the rest of the article. Which paragraphs are concerned with *pageantry* and which are concerned with *serious political business*?

2

How quickly can you find answers to these questions about the Queen's speech?

a Who writes the speech?

b Who reads the speech?

c Whose views does the speech represent?

d Where exactly is the speech made?

e Who is present while the speech is made?

f On what day of the week is the speech made?

g In which month?

h At what time?

3

a Read the list of events below and try to put them in order.

  1 The Speaker of the House of Commons, the Prime Minister and the Leader of the main opposition party lead the other MPs to the House of Lords.

  2 The Queen puts on her ceremonial dress and crown.

  3 The Queen goes to the throne in the chamber of the House of Lords.

  4 Members of the House of Lords, in their ceremonial dress, greet the Queen on her arrival there.

  5 The Queen reads her speech at 11 am.

  6 The Queen sends her messenger to the House of Commons to call MPs to the House of Lords.

  7 The Royal Family drive from Buckingham Palace to the House of Lords.

  8 The door is closed as the Queen's messenger approaches so he knocks on it three times and then enters.

b Now read the paragraphs concerned with *pageantry* and check your order.

4

What do you think of this ceremony? Which of these words do you think describes it best?

a beautiful

b traditional

c historic

d silly

e pompous

Tomorrow's ceremonial Opening of Parliament is not just a chance to don ermine robes and pipe up the pomp and circumstance.

TOMORROW the Queen will open Parliament for what could be its last session before a General Election. The opening ceremony will be a mixture of pageantry and serious political business. Once the Queen has taken her seat on the throne in the House of Lords she will read a speech outlining the new laws the Government is planning to make in the forthcoming parliamentary year.

But the title "Queen's Speech" is misleading. It is not really the Queen's Speech at all, but the Government's. It is prepared by the Prime Minister and his or her colleagues and is read by the Queen. It is not an expression of the Queen's own views.

This year's Queen's Speech is unlikely to contain as many bills as in previous years. This is because the Government may want to cut short the parliamentary year and call a General Election. The main issues are likely to be a criminal justice bill to change the criminal law, and a "green" bill to clean up the environment.

Other measures expected to be in the Queen's Speech are new laws to bring privately financed toll-roads and new rules to ease traffic congestion in London.

The right royal State Opening of Parliament

THE Queen's Speech always takes place on a Wednesday in November, in the House of Lords at 11am. It is the centrepiece of the State Opening of Parliament. This is the event where the Queen puts on her glittering ceremonial dress and crown and speaks from a throne, watched by her husband, other members of her family and assembled Lords and MPs. The ceremony begins with a procession of carriages from Buckingham Palace, bearing the Queen and her family. On arrival at the House of Lords, she makes her way to the chamber, where the throne is situated, to make her speech. This has been the practice since 1536. She is greeted in the Lords by the peers and peeresses in ermine robes. In the Commons, MPs are waiting to be summoned, dressed slightly less glamorously.

It is a long-standing tradition that the Monarch never enters the House of Commons. Instead he or she uses a messenger, the Gentleman Usher of the Black Rod, usually known as Black Rod, to summon MPs to the Lords.

As Black Rod approaches the Commons chamber across the Central Lobby of the Houses of Parliament, the door of the Commons is traditionally slammed in his face, a custom which dates from the time Charles I tried to arrest five MPs in 1642.

Black Rod then raps three times on the door with his ebony stick and the door is opened. He proceeds, bowing all the time to the table in front of the Speaker, who maintains order in the debates in the Commons, to summon MPs to the Lords. The Speaker is elected by the House of Commons from among its members. Speakers are MPs, but once elected, they must resign from their party. The current Speaker is Betty Boothroyd. The Speaker, followed by the Prime Minister and the Leader of the Opposition, then make their way into the Lords, followed by MPs walking two by two, to hear the speech.

Section C

1

Look at the table

a Which country has . . . ?
  1 the highest percentage of women in government
  2 the lowest percentage of women in government
b What might these figures suggest about . . . ?
  1 the political system of each country
  2 the role of women in society
c Why do you think there are relatively few women in politics in many countries?

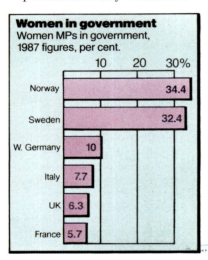

Women in government
Women MPs in government, 1987 figures, per cent.

Country	Per cent
Norway	34.4
Sweden	32.4
W. Germany	10
Italy	7.7
UK	6.3
France	5.7

LABOUR'S LOST MPs

PATRICIA HEWITT

Deputy director of the Institute for Public Policy Research: formerly Neil Kinnock's press and broadcasting secretary. She began trying for a Labour seat in the late 1970s — "looking for a seat takes an enormous amount of time, and money, too, if you're travelling a lot".

She was finally chosen to fight Leicester East for Labour in the 1983 elections. "I was planning to have a child after the elections — looking back I don't know how I imagined I was going to cope if Labour had won the seat."

At the time she was general secretary of the National Council of Civil Liberties and driving up from London to Leicester two evenings a week. "Even without children, I was leading such a pressured life — and my partner was doing the same as a Labour councillor — that it did put a strain on our relationship."

She took a conscious decision not to look for a seat this time round. "I've got two small children and I don't want to lead that kind of life."

MARGARET HODGE

Leader of Islington council. She has not been short of invitations from constituencies asking her to stand. "It's been a hard decision; the next logical step is from local to national politics and I would love to be part of a Labour government influencing change. But it's simply inconsistent with family life, and I have four children who mean a lot to me.

"It does make me angry that the only way up the political ladder is to work at it 24 hours a day, seven days a week. That's not just inappropriate for a woman who has to look after children or relatives, it's inappropriate for any normal person.

"The way Parliament functions doesn't attract me very much. MPs can seem terribly self-obsessed, more interested in their latest media appearance than in creating change."

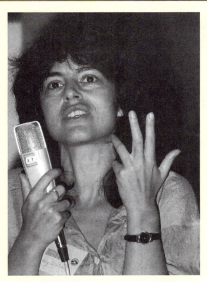

MARY KALDOR

Senior research fellow at the Science Policy Research Unit of Sussex University, and former foreign policy adviser to Labour. She was shortlisted for Hackney and Dulwich in 1981, and remembers "masses of meetings, many of which were boring, and endlessly having to be nice to people".

Her youngest child was two years old at the time. "I was very well-equipped with baby minders and a nice understanding husband, but what on earth is the point of having children if you're not going to see them?"

She was ambivalent about the idea of becoming an MP; the whole process seemed to her "entirely about competitiveness and being in the limelight, giving you no time to think honestly about your political views". She was too ill with hepatitis to go to Hackney's final selection meeting; in retrospect, she is not sorry. "Building links with eastern Europe through the peace movement was more exciting than anything I could ever have done as an MP."

2

Read these opinions about women and Parliament. Which do you agree with? Which do you disagree with? Give reasons.

a 'Women don't have a fair chance of becoming MPs.'

b 'If a woman has got young children, she should look after them. That's more important than becoming an MP.'

c 'I don't think Parliament's that important anyway. You can change things more easily if you work outside of Parliament.'

d 'There's a need to change the way Parliament works to make it easier for women to become effective MPs.'

3

a Look at the title of the article. What do you think *lost* means here?

b Read the article and see if you were right.

4

Read the article again.

a What political party do the women belong to?

b Have they got children?

c Have they ever stood for election to Parliament? Were they successful?

5

Which profile(s) mention(s) . . . ?

a the long hours worked by all MPs

b the selection process as a political candidate

c the attraction of being in the government

d the attraction of working outside the government

6

Work in a group of three. Choose one woman each.

a Which of the opinions expressed in **2** would she agree with? Which would she disagree with?

b Imagine you are the three women. Discuss your views of women in politics.

P*roject*

Work in a group to produce a poster on the elected national assembly in your country.

a *Research facts and figures and produce a factfile.*

b *Find out about the political calendar and parliamentary ceremonies. Write an article using photographs from magazines or newspapers.*

c *Write an article about the history of parliament in your country. What changes have take place? What are major areas of discussion today?*

d *Investigate the role of women in politics in your country and record your findings.*

A green and pleasant land?

Britain, like the rest of Europe, is trying to clean itself up. The recycling of paper, glass, and plastic has increased dramatically. Nevertheless, the question remains: how 'green' is Britain?

Section A

1
Read this article quickly. Explain the title.

2
Now read the first paragraph again and complete this table.

date	population
....	1 billion
1975	....
2030	....

3
Give three examples of ways in which the increase in human population has hurt the environment.

NO TIME TO WASTE

For hundreds of thousands of years, the human race has thrived in Earth's environment. By 1800 there were 1 billion people on the planet. That number had doubled by 1975. If current birth rates hold, the present population of 5.1 billion will double again in 40 years. The frightening irony is that our success as an organism could condemn the Earth as a human habitat. We have upset nature's sensitive equilibrium – disgorging noxious gases into the atmosphere, dumping toxic waste into rivers and oceans and tearing up the countryside to accommodate our rubbish.

What would happen if we did nothing about the threat to the Earth?

Computers project that an accumulation of carbon dioxide in the atmosphere could drive up the Earth's average temperature from 3°F to 9°F by the middle of the next century. Sea levels would rise by several feet, flooding coastal areas and ruining vast tracts of farmland. Huge areas would be infertile and become uninhabitable. Water contamination could lead to shortages of safe drinking water.

In the last decade of the 20th century, we are at a crucial turning point. The actions of those now living will determine the future and possibly the very survival of the species. Spurred by poverty, population growth, ill advised policies and simple greed, humanity is at war with the plants, animals and elements that make up the planet and provide for our continued existence.

We only have a few years to attempt to turn things around. We must review our wasteful, careless ways; we must consume less, recycle more, conserve energy and adapt our lifestyles for the sake of those who will inherit the planet.

RECYCLING

- **regenerates the environment**
- **conserves our resources**
- **reduces pollution and litter**
- **reduces acid rain**
- **reduces the need for landfill sites**
- **cuts energy costs**
- **generates jobs**
- **engenders a sense of community pride**
- **creates profitable industry**
- **provides funds for charity**

4

Read the second paragraph again and answer the question in the subheading.

5

Read the rest of the article and answer these questions:

a Why does the writer say 'we are at a crucial turning point'?

b In what way is the conflict between humanity and the environment like a war?

6

Match these words and their meanings in this article.

habitat	*motivated*
equilibrium	*areas*
toxic	*increase*
project	*environment*
drive up	*badly-thought out*
tracts	*poisonous*
spurred	*balance*
ill-advised	*predict*

Factfile | **Conservation and pollution**

1
In 1990 British consumers threw away 6 million tonnes of paper, 2 million tonnes of glass and £35 million worth of aluminium.

2
Only 4% of recyclable material is actually recycled.

3
The estimated annual value of materials which are thrown away in Britain is £750 million per annum.

4
In Britain there is one bottle bank for every 14,000 people. In France and Germany the figure is one bottle bank for every 2,000.

5
At the end of 1990 80% of petrol stations sold unleaded petrol. In 1988 the figure was only 4%.

6
Emissions from lead from petrol fell by more than 50% between 1975 and 1988, despite an increase in petrol consumption of over 7 million tonnes.

7
90% of British rubbish is tipped into holes in the ground called landfill sites. There are 5,000 such landfill sites in Britain today.

7

Work with a partner. Look at the points mentioned about recycling. Which *three* are the most important?

8

a Which fact do you find the most surprising?

b Which situation needs the most urgent action?

c Which fact arouses the most optimism?

9

Can you explain the meaning of this logo?

Project |

In groups organise a recycling project.
Think about these questions:

a *What are you goint to recycle – paper, plastic, tins, bottles?*

b *How can you encourage people to recycle – produce an explanatory leaflet or poster, organise a competition?*

c *How are the things going to be collected – a central collection point, volunteer collections, house-to-house collection?*

d *How can other people be made to help – form a committee, talk to other students, persuade shopkeepers, tell the municipal authorities?*

e *What other events can be organised to help the project – a sale of old books, clothes or records; a sponsored walk, bike ride or run; a collection in the town?*

Section B

CHILDREN WHO play in the sea at Blackpool run more than five times the risk of developing symptoms of sewage poisoning than those who stay on the beach, according to scientists.

Research findings published by a team from Lancaster University today provide some of the clearest evidence to date of the health dangers posed by untreated sewage in sea water.

The university's Environmental Epidemiology Research Unit interviewed the parents of more than 900 children, aged six to 11, on the beach at Blackpool last summer. In follow-up interviews 10 to 14 days later, parents were asked several questions, including whether their children had suffered from any of a list of 29 symptoms.

After statistical analysis to eliminate the possibility of error, the unit discovered that the 455 children in the sample who had had contact with the sea ran a significantly higher risk of contracting symptoms of disease associated with sewage pollution.

The children who went in the sea were five times more likely to be affected by diarrhoea than those on the beach, and three times more likely to suffer from vomiting. Other symptoms included itchy skin, fever, lack of energy and loss of appetite.

EVIDENCE is mounting that Blackpool townspeople are at risk from illnesses linked to sewage pollution of the sea, even if they do not swim in it.

According to a Blackpool GP, increasing numbers of residents are suffering from gastro-intestinal illnesses and sinusitis, which he believes are caused by sewage pollution.

Worry over the health threat has prompted Lancashire County Council to sponsor a study by Lancaster University into the connection between ill-health in children living on the Fylde coast and pollution.

The GP, Dr Martin Lucking, said that in recent years, increasing numbers of his patients have suffered gastro-intestinal illnesses and sinusitis during periods of strong on-shore winds bringing moisture from the sea.

'This happened in 1988 and late on in 1989. It is unacceptable that this is going on on our doorstep.'

1
Look at the photograph. Read the first paragraph of both articles. Where was the photograph taken?

2
Now read the two articles. Which article was published first?

3
a Write a headline for each article.
b Work in a group. Compare your headlines. Choose the best ones.

4

Are these statements about Blackpool true or false? Correct the false statements.

a Children are not in danger as long as they stay out of the sea.

b Lancashire County Council carried out a survey into the connection between ill-health and pollution from the sea.

c The pollution in the sea is caused by untreated sewage.

d The major illness that children suffered was diarrhoea.

e Children also complained of headaches.

f According to Dr Lucking, the number of patients suffering from pollution-related illnesses has increased recently.

5

a How would you react to the findings of the report if you were a . . . ?

  1 Blackpool parent
  2 tourist
  3 hotel owner

b Now read the torn out comments from the newspaper. Match each comment with the person who made it.

  1 John Hall, Director of Tourism for Blackpool
  2 Louise Ellman, Leader of Lancashire County Council
  3 Dr Martin Lucking, Blackpool GP

6

a Work in a group. What do you think should be done?

b Write a letter to one of the Blackpool newspapers expressing your point of view.

'This is seriously going to affect our trade. The constant spotlight on Blackpool's beaches means we will pay the price and if you take away tourism Blackpool is nothing.'

'We have known since Victorian times that there is a link between sewage and ill-health and I would say it is up to the authorities to prove otherwise.'

'The water authority's proposals are inadequate. We need firm plans for the short term. There is too much anecdotal evidence of people in this area becoming ill. It must be treated seriously.'

Section C

HERITAGE COASTS

What are Heritage Coasts?

Over two-thirds of the coastline of England and Wales has already been built-up and threats hang over much of the rest. In the last 20 years two major attempts have been made to conserve what remains of our unspoilt seaside. In 1965 the National Trust launched a fund-raising campaign called Enterprise Neptune, the aim being to acquire 900 miles of undeveloped coastline in England and Wales. Over half this target has already been achieved and the scheme is to be relaunched in April to continue the task. In 1970 the Countryside Commission set up the Heritage Coast scheme, with very similar aims: that is, to protect the best natural coastal scenery in England and Wales (Scotland has its own coastal conservation scheme) and to encourage people to enjoy it without changing its character.

Most of the 40 or so Heritage Coasts originally planned have now been defined, and the first stage of the project is virtually complete. The future of some sections of Heritage Coast is reasonably well assured because they coincide with National Parks, nature reserves, National Trust land, etc. But in other areas everything depends on the continuing goodwill and support of landowners and local authorities, and on the co-operation of the public when visiting the coast. Many conflicting interests are involved, and resolving them all is no easy task.

Nearly one-third of the coastline of England and Wales has been defined as Heritage Coast – 850 miles of some of the finest coastal scenery to be found anywhere in Europe.

1
Read the article *What are Heritage Coasts*? Answer the question in the title.

2
Find the names of three countries and two national organisations in the article.

3
Complete the summary notes on the right by filling in information on the dotted lines.

4
Look through the unit. What is being done to keep Britain *a green and pleasant land*?

attempts to conserve coast:
1965 ....
.... Heritage Coast (HC)

common aims:
1 to protect coastal scenery
2 ....

Heritage Coasts well-publicised = those that coincide with ....

Other areas dependant on ....

'A sort of national property'

Britain is a small country with beautiful and varied countryside, but it is constantly under threat. How have Britain's national parks helped preserve the countryside?

Section A

1

a What is a national park?
b Can you name any national parks in your country?

2

Read the first paragraph of the article.

a Which of these questions about national parks does the first paragraph answer?

1 Where was the first national park?
2 When was the first national park set up in England?
3 How many national parks are there in England and Wales?
4 Which is the most popular national park?

b Answer the questions.

3

Read the first paragraph again.

a Choose the correct sentence ending. Wordsworth thought that . . . .

1 everyone should have the right to enjoy the Lake District
2 only people who can appreciate the Lake District should have the right to enjoy it

There have been national parks in the United States for more than a century. Long before that, William Wordsworth, the great English poet, suggested that his native Lake District should become 'a sort of national property, in which every man has a right and interest who has an eye to perceive and a heart to enjoy'. Nevertheless, it was not until 1949 that the first national park in England and Wales was set up. Now there are ten national parks which cover 13,600 km² of England and Wales – 9% of the total land area.

The first aim of establishing national parks is to provide protection for the outstanding countryside they contain; the second aim is to provide opportunities for people to have access to them and enjoy them.

The Lake District in the _____ of England is the largest national park. It is popular with walkers, canoeists, cyclists, sailors, and climbers. Although it is quite compact – it is only _____ km from east to west – it has some of the most spectacular and varied scenery in Britain. It has Windermere, at 16.4 kilometres the longest lake in England, and Scafell Pike, at 1000 metres the highest mountain in England. Also in the Lake District is Sty Head, the wettest place in Britain. More than 4000 millimetres of rain a year fall on Sty Head!

The Lake District was largely unknown until the end of the 18th century. Then the works of writers based in the Lake District, such as Wordsworth and Coleridge, attracted visitors to the grandeur of the Lakes. At first only a trickle of artists and poets came to marvel at the grim mountains and the idyllic lakes. But over the years that trickle has become a flood, until the Lake District is now one of the most popular tourist destinations in Britain. In 1990 a total of _____ tourist nights (one night spent by one person) were recorded in the Lake District.

4

Read the second paragraph.

a National parks have two aims. What are they?
b Can you think of any situations where these two aims might be in conflict?

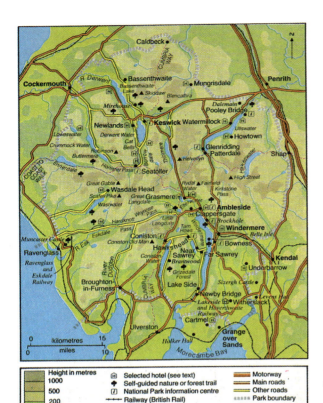

Height in metres		
1000	Ⓗ Selected hotel (see text)	Motorway
500	♣ Self-guided nature or forest trail	Main roads
200	Ⓘ National Park information centre	Other roads
100	+--+ Railway (British Rail)	Park boundary
0	——— Railway (private)	Military training area

5

Use the factfile and map to complete the third and fourth paragraphs of the article on the previous page.

6

Which of these descriptions best fits the Lake District?

a large, beautiful and interesting
b small, scenic and popular
c small, mountainous and diverse

7

Look at the map again.

a Read the four descriptions below and find the places on the map. Choose from this list of places.
Derwent Water   Great Gable   Hawkshead
Scafell Pike   Skiddaw   Windermere

  1 Small village between Windermere and Coniston, where Wordsworth went to school.
  2 The longest of the English lakes.
  3 Mountain just to the north of Wastwater.
  4 Mountain just north of Keswick.

b Write similar descriptions of the other two places in the list.

Factfile | National Parks

1
National parks are not owned by the nation. Most of the land is still in private hands.

2
There are ten national parks in England and Wales. There are no national parks in Scotland. Instead there are three regional parks and 40 'national scenic areas', covering about 13% of the total land area of Scotland.

3
There are 11 forest parks in Great Britain, which are administered by the Forestry Commission.

4
The cost of administering national parks in England and Wales in 1990 was £18.5 million

5
Approximately 250,000 people live in the national parks in England and Wales.

6
The resident population of the Lake District is 41,000.

7
National parks in England and Wales receive 90 million visits a year.

8
In 1990 14 million tourist nights were recorded in the Lake District National Park in the north west of England.

Project |

Work in a group to write an article about national parks in your country.
Think about these questions:
a *How many national parks are there in your country?*
b *Where are they?*
c *What kind of environment do they protect – mountains, coastline, marshes, forests?*
d *What restrictions (if any) are placed on tourists?*
e *Who pays for the maintenance of the parks?*

Section B

1

3

2

4

1

Look at the photographs (1–4) and captions (a–d) from a brochure about Lake District holidays. Match the photographs with the captions.

a There is excellent fishing in the rivers and lakes.

b Many young people first learn to canoe on the quiet waters of Lakeland.

c There are courses in painting for those who would like to capture the beauty of the Lake District landscape.

d Pony-trekking is a popular activity, especially for children.

2

Work with a partner. Which of these activities would you choose to do and why?

THERE WAS a time when the sights and sounds from the crest of Helvellyn were savoured only by sturdy walkers, determined folk with time and an easy pace.

Now determined cyclists, who pedal up the 3,118ft mountain, have established rights of play in the Lake District.

The Lake District National Park authority has decided to welcome them informally, much to the displeasure of many walkers, by staging the first mountain bike "teach-in" within a national park. Donald Angus, one of the park's rangers, will hold special courses on the "considerate use of mountain bikes".

Many walkers accuse the riders of being aggressive and abusive. The riders, who seem reasonable and polite, say the walkers want to keep places such as the Lake District to themselves and do not like intruders.

Anne Barnett, a housewife in Ambleside, has turned a hobby into a successful Lakeland mountain bike hire business, with an enormous increase in users over the past year.

"Providing people behave and act sensibly, including

A welcome in the hillsides for considerate bike riders

the walkers, there is no reason for conflict. The bikers are ambassadors for cycling and do not want trouble. They just want to enjoy crossing the hills in a different, fun way," she says.

The National Trust, however, is none too pleased with the upsurge. Neil Allinson, an upland access adviser, says it is "watchful" of the craze.

He added: "We do feel they can do far more damage to the environment than walkers." The bikes are somewhat alien and we cannot say cyclists and walkers in this situation are the best of bedfellows."

Eddie Hibbert, secretary of the Lake District Ramblers' Association, is blunt about mountain bike riders. "I do not feel they should be there at all. Many do break the law and they are aggressive."

3

Work with a partner. Look at the headline, of the article. How do you think *considerate bike-riders* should behave in the Lake District?

4

Read the article. What jobs do these people do?
a Donald Angus   b Anne Barnett
c Neil Allinson   d Eddie Hibbert

5

Work in a group of four. Imagine you are each one of the people mentioned above.

a Read the article carefully. Would you, in your role, agree or disagree with these statements?

 1 Mountain bikes should be banned on the hillsides.

 2 Mountain-bikers do more damage to the hills than walkers do.
 3 Walkers are selfish in opposing mountain bikes.
 4 There is no reason for conflict between bikers and walkers.
 5 The use of mountain bikes should be carefully monitored.

b Discuss the issue of biking in the Lake District. Don't forget to introduce yourself and say something about your job.

6

What do you really think? Should the hills be left to walkers or should mountain-bikers be allowed on them too?

Section C

1

Read the three extracts.

a Who was the *Poet of the Lakes*?
b What was his sister's name?

> I wandered lonely as a cloud
> That floats on high o'er vales and hills,
> When all at once I saw a crowd,
> A host, of golden daffodils;
> Beside the lake, beneath the trees,
> Fluttering and dancing in the breeze.
>
> Continuous as the stars that shine
> And twinkle on the milky way,
> They stretch in never-ending line
> Along the margin of a bay:
> Ten thousand saw I at a glance,
> Tossing their heads in sprightly dance.

Poet of the Lakes

William Wordsworth (1770–1850) was the greatest English poet of his day. Born in Cockermouth, he went to school in Hawkshead and his most creative years were spent in Grasmere, where he lived with his sister Dorothy at Dove Cottage. Although he won many honours and was made Poet Laureate in 1843, Wordsworth always remained attached to his homeland: he was always a poet of the Lakes.

Wordsworth's most famous poem is the poem we now call Daffodils. *In this untitled work the poet describes something he and his sister saw while walking along the shores of Ullswater. Dorothy recorded the incident in her 'Journal' and William used these notes when he was writing his poem.*

When we were in the woods beyond Gowbarrow Park, we saw a few daffodils close to the water-side. We fancied that the lake had floated the seeds ashore, and that the little colony had so sprung up. But as we went along there were more and yet more; and at last, under the boughs of the trees, we saw that there was a long belt of them along the shore, about the breadth of a country turnpike road. I never saw daffodils so beautiful. They grew among the mossy stones around and about them; some rested their heads upon these stones, as on a pillow, for weariness; and the rest tossed and reeled and danced, and seemed as if they verily laughed with the wind, that blew upon them over the lake; they looked so gay, ever glancing, ever changing.

2

a Find these phrases in Dorothy's description.
  1 '. . . rested their heads upon these stones, as on a pillow, for weariness . . .'
  2 '. . . tossed and reeled and danced . . .'
  3 '. . . they verily laughed with the wind . . .'
  4 '. . . they looked so gay'

Now complete this statement:
She writes about the daffodils as if they were
. . . .

b 1 Does William make the same comparison?
  2 What does he compare the daffodils to?
  3 What does he compare himself to?

3

a How many verses are there in *Daffodils*? How many lines are there in each verse?
b Look at the last word on each line of the poem. Which words have the same sound? Is there a pattern? Is the rhyming pattern the same in each verse?

4

a Read Dorothy's Journal entry and William's poem again.
b Work with a partner. Which of these words would you use to describe Dorothy's journal entry? Which describe Wiliam's poem?

beautiful comprehensible imaginative
natural vivid descriptive

Helping the hungry

People in Britain contribute millions of pounds a year to charities such as Comic Relief *and* Oxfam, *which help relieve hunger in developing countries. The government also has a massive aid programme. But how is the money spent?*

Section A

1

a Look at the photograph and the headline. What do you think might be happening?

b Read the article and find out what you can about *Charity Projects*.

c Now look at the date of the newspaper article and read the first sentence of the article. When exactly is *Red Nose Day*?

2

Read the article carefully.

a What is the distinction between *Red Nose Day, Comic Relief* and *Charity Projects*?

b How exactly does *Comic Relief* raise money on *Red Nose Day*? Find two distinct ways mentioned in the article.

c Give examples of the things people have promised to do on *Red Nose Day*. What do they have in common? Which do you think is the silliest? Which would you least like to do?

d What is the aim of the *Comic Relief* films?

e Compare the two pieces of film described in the article. Which do the people watching think is good? Which do they think is bad? Why?

f What three things does *Comic Relief* want to avoid in its films?

10/3/91

The hard-nosed

By **William Leith**

WITH SIX days to go to Red Nose Day, everybody is keeping a straight face in the Comic Relief fund-raising office in Acton. This is serious work. "He's got a talking nose," says one woman. "Yes. Any size we want it." Another woman is shouting across the room: "No, those noses are not for general use – they're not the ones to be dipped into. Those are the Ascension Island noses." The first woman puts her telephone down and resumes an earlier conversation. "Jelly in the underpants," she says. "Different flavours of jelly in the underpants."

The previous Red Nose Day, in 1988, raised £27m. That target looks hard to beat. But the recent response has been good; 2,300 formal applications have been made for the "Nose That Glows" competition, and 50,000 informal ones are expected.

The ideas nearly all involve mild humiliation, as if people want to atone for the sin of being from a rich country. The computer print-out of the schemes, four inches thick, reads: "Sitting in a bath full of custard"; "sitting in a bath of baked beans", "dyeing my hair bright green", "eating all the vegetables I hate for one week", "filling wellingtons with custard".

Invicta Plastics, the Leicester company that designs the noses, has created a new one, with a face on the front and hands at the side. This will be difficult to pirate. The red nose black economy, buoyant in recent years, is expected to collapse. "And

we've come up with a new idea," says Annie Williams, in charge of fund-raising. "The building nose. It's three feet across and you stick it on the outside of your house, or your office."

The building nose costs £80 from Invicta and £1,000 from Comic Relief. This year, there are 9.3 million facial noses, 2.5 milion car noses, and 1,000 building noses. Woolworth, whch has spent £93,000 on the noses, has exclusive retail rights.

In the West End, at Charity Projects, the Comic Relief head office, Jane Tewson, director of the project, Kevin Cahill, director of education, and Will Day, in charge of Africa, watch rough-cuts of the Comic Relief films, starring Griff Rhys-Jones and Tony Richardson, about what will happen to your money if you part with it on Red Nose Day.

One film depicts Richardson, on location in Central Africa, with some thin Africans and some small bowls of grain and nuts. "Enjoy your supper," he says. "That'll have to go," says Will Day. "One thing we don't do is make people feel guilty."

There are two more things Comic Relief is keen to avoid: spending money on emergencies rather than long-term projects and depicting the needy in a patronising way. What Comic Relief wants is optimism; to give potential donors the idea that giving will do lasting good. "In the next three months we could have a wing-ding spending spree," says

3

a Look up a definition of *hard-nosed* in a dictionary.

b Why do you think William Leith chose to use this phrase in the headline?

c Find an example of *hard-nosed* behaviour in the article.

business of Red Nose Day

Day. "But in six months' time you couldn't tell the money had been spent at all."

One film is about a man in Kenya who has been taught to test people's eyes and perform cataract operations; it ends with the song "I Can See Clearly Now". Everybody nods and says, "That's fantastic."

After 10 years of compassion-fatigue, of Band Aid, Live Aid and Telethons, the typical Westerner is tooled up with anti-charity arguments. Many don't give because they think charity defers government reform. "What they don't realise" says Mr Day, "is that the government of an African country has very little economic control. The prices for its goods are set in the West."

This year's Comic Relief will be gentler and more optimistic; it will try to make you smile rather than flinch. But those on the receiving end, whose lives may be saved, would still flinch if they knew the bowl of rice that saved them was the result of a Westerner spending a couple of hours in a bath full of baked beans.

Section B

1

Work in a group.

a Now that you have completed Section A decide if these statements are true or false.

   1 Much of the money raised goes to help people in Africa.
   2 *Comic Relief* prefers to involve local people in its projects.
   3 Water and health schemes have received money from *Comic Relief*.

b Now look at the diagram and check your answers.

2

a Work in pairs. One person is a spokesperson for *Charity Projects* and the other is a television interviewer. Use the information given in the flow-chart and Section A to answer these questions. Practise the interview with your partner and then swap over roles.

   1 Where does the money collected on *Red Nose Day* go? Does it all go to Africa?
   2 Which British charities working in Africa benefit most from *Red Nose Day*?
   3 Is the money spent mostly on large-scale projects?
   4 What is *Charity Projects* looking for when it chooses projects to support?
   5 Can you give us some examples of the kind of project *Charity Projects* supports?
   6 Would you like to make one final point about *Comic Relief*?

How the money gets to Africa

This is what happens to all the money collected on Red Nose Day

Charity Projects

All the money from Red Nose Day and Comic Relief is controlled by a parent charity called Charity Projects. For every pound given, one third goes to charities working in the UK, two thirds goes to charities working in Africa.

UK registered charities at work in Africa

Thousands of charities apply for funds by submitting proposals for specific projects. Generally one third goes to Oxfam, one third to Save the Children and the rest to other charities.

In choosing proposals Charity Projects looks for cost effectiveness, involvement of the local community and sustainability. It avoids large expensive projects and encourages those that create work locally. These are the sort of projects it likes to support.

URBAN
Sanitation, health programmes in squatter areas

WATER & HEALTH
Providing training and support

TREES
Rain forest protection, erosion control

EMERGENCIES
Water, shelter, transport, health

AGRICULTURE
Support of co-operative groups

DISABILITY
Working with disabled groups

LOCAL GROUPS
Support development, eg. care and adoption

3

Look quickly at the article opposite, *'Axes drawn in the mud'*.

a Who wrote the article?
b What do you already know about this person?
c Is the article written as a letter, a diary or a news item?

4

a Read the headlines. Where did the writer go? Why?
b 1 What are *refugees*?
   2 Read Saturday's entry. How many *refugees* are there in Malawi? Where are they from?
c What do you expect the rest of the article to contain?
d Read the article quickly and check your predictions.

5

Read the article again.

a What is the name of Jane's colleague from London?

b On which day did these things happen?

  1 They met an engineer from the *Save the Children Fund.*

  2 Fiona became ill.

  3 They drove along the border.

  4 They saw disabled people in clinics.

  5 Fiona spent a day at the Hospital.

6

Sunday

a What do Jane and Fiona see on their right and on their left?

Monday

b Why does Jane sleep badly? Why does Rob sleep well?

Wednesday

c Why are the girl's elbows 'thickly calloused'?

d Why does Jane mention the tea-pickers? And the pencil?

Thursday

e Why did the people at the *Save the Children* office smile at first?

Friday

f Why did Jane have a sleepless night?

g The mother of 16 children sympathises with Jane because she hasn't got any children. How do you think Jane feels about her?

7

Find expressions in Jane's diary which mean the following:

a very early (Sunday)

b enjoy (Monday)

c very impressed (Wednesday)

d experienced people (Thursday)

e I almost faint with shock (Friday)

Axes drawn in the mud

Jane Tewson, of Comic Relief, travels to Malawi to assess refugee needs

Saturday At last – airborne and on the way to Lilongwe, Malawi's capital (courtesy of British Airways), leaving the frenetic world of Red Noses and drizzle for 100°F. Around 800,000 Mozambicans have sought sanctuary in Malawi from the war in their country. We are going to see how aid can best be given.

Sunday At the crack of dawn we leave for the south of the country. A dramatic introduction to the refugee situation comes when our road suddenly turns into the Mozambique border. To our right lies forested land; to our left, bare hillsides covered with thousands of tiny thatched huts, each of which houses 12 people.

Monday To Mankhokwe refugee camp, where we meet Rob, the Save the Children Fund water engineer. The camp, which houses 80,000 people, lies beside a river. Rob points at it and says: "Would you fancy drinking five parts water, four parts animal waste and one part mud, stirred gently?"

We spend the night with Rob. It is so hot that the candles droop in elegant curves. The fan blows heat at us like a hair dryer. The night is hell, mosquitoes humming. I'm drenched in sweat. Rob says he slept well because it was a cooler night.

Wednesday We visit rural clinics with a group called Malawi Against Polio (Map). In a morning we see people's lives being changed in a simple, dignified manner. The clinic waiting-room is a cloth and timber shack with a clean concrete floor, upon which sit 50 or more disabled people. Many lost their limbs either from land mines or infected wounds.

I was bowled over by the human adaptability. One man had one of his legs wrapped behind his neck and the other hanging in a sling in front, which enabled him to speed along on his bottom, propelled with his hands. A large girl with withered legs walked on her thickly calloused elbows. Her father, a subsistence farmer, was committed to sending her to school, but because of her increasing weight was unable to carry her the two kilometres. Map agreed to try to get her a wheelchair by the start of the school year.

We drive back through tea plantations that go on and on and on. Tea-pickers earn as little as 40 tambala a day – that's just over 10p. A pencil costs 95 tambala.

Thursday Back to Lilongwe. The hardened hands at the Save the Children office smile as my companion, Fiona dashes off to the loo every few minutes. Faces become more serious when her temperature soars to 104°F. At the Kamuzu Central Hospital cerebral malaria is diagnosed.

Friday After a sleepless night I visit the hospital. My heart stops when a coffin is wheeled out of the ward. Fiona isn't in her bed, but when I go back to the ward office she greets me, looking gaunt. The treatment worked.

Later, I remember it's my 32nd birthday. I am talking to a woman of my age who has had 16 children, 11 of whom have survived. She pours sympathy on me when I say that I haven't had babies yet.

Monday We arrive back. My visit has reinforced my determination to put as much as possible into Red Nose Day 3 in March. We cannot be distracted. At least 20 million Africans face starvation this year.

8

Imagine you are Jane. You have to write a report on your visit to Malawi.

a Discuss with a partner what projects should be supported and what aid should be given.

b Write your report, making recommendations based on what you saw during your visit.

Section C

1

a Read the factfile. Can you guess which numbers below fit which spaces?

1,500   82   41   27   17

Factfile | **Overseas Aid**

1
In 1991 Britain gave 300 billion in overseas aid.

2
The top 400 British charities raise more than £..................... million a year for overseas aid.

3
The first *Red Nose Day* in 1988 raised £27 million and in 1991 *Comic Relief* raised another £..................... million for aid to charities working in Britain and Africa.

4
The largest British charity that deals with overseas aid is *Oxfam*. In 1990 it had an income of £52 million, most of which, £..................... million, came from voluntary contributions from members of the public.

5
Most off the money *Oxfam* raises goes directly to overseas aid and education: .... pence in every £1.

6
Oxfam also raises money through its shops. *Oxfam* shops sell second hand clothes as well as handicrafts (baskets, rugs, bowls) produced in developing countries. There are now over 800 *Oxfam* shops in Britain which raise more than £..................... million for overseas aid.

7
In the past few years there have been a number of television appeals for help with charitable causes. In 1990 the charity *Children in Need* raised £24 million as the result of a day-long television appeal.

Project |

Work in a group to plan a fund-raising campaign.

a *Choose a charity or particular project (real or imaginary) that you would like to support.*
b *Decide how you are going to raise money.*
c *Devise advertisements and write newspaper articles/publicity for your campaign.*
d *Present your campaign to the rest of the class.*

How European is Britain?

Britain is an island. It is also part of Europe. Are the British becoming true Europeans? If so, why can't they speak anything else but English?

Section A

1

Work with a partner and discuss these questions.

a How do people from your country view the British?

b How does their view compare with the view expressed in the cartoon?

c How often do you meet British people in your country?

d How do you get on with them?

e Can they generally speak your language?

f How do they behave? How would you describe them?

g How 'European' are the British?

2

Work with a partner. Look quickly at the two texts, below and opposite.

a Which text is . . . ?

  1 from a TV magazine
  2 an advertisement from a newspaper

b Who are these texts addressed to?

c Who paid for the advertisement?

3

Read the texts carefully. What does the text 'Sachs' unspeakable thoughts!' tell you about . . . ?

a Andrew Sachs' background

b a TV role he used to play

c a programme that he's about to appear in

4

a Find the words *peeved* and *beleaguered* in 'Sachs' unspeakable thoughts!'. What do you think they mean?

b Compare your definitions with the definition in a dictionary.

c Why do you think Andrew Sachs was *peeved*? Why was Manuel *beleaguered*?

5

Work with a partner. Read the text 'There's no need . . .,' again.

a Do you agree with the idea expressed in the headline of the text? Is it a sensible attitude to take to people who don't speak your language?

b Why do you think the advertisers chose this headline?

c Why do you think the advertisers use Spanish towards the end of the text? Can you explain what it means in English?

d What exactly is the message of the advertisement? Choose the best summary.

  1 There's no need for British businessmen and women to learn a foreign language, because everyone speaks English anyway.

  2 Other European businessmen and women spend more time and money on learning foreign languages than we do. As a result, they're beating us to good business opportunities.

  3 In the European Community, language skill is going to be very important in business. British businessmen and women need to change their attitude towards foreign languages or they will lose their share of the market.

Sachs' unspeakable thoughts!

'When I first came to England as a child, all I could say was: "I'm sorry, but I do not understand you. I am a little German boy,"' explains Andrew Sachs. 'I was a little bit peeved at that – I thought I was a *big* German boy!'

Andrew went on to play the beleaguered Spanish waiter Manuel in *Fawlty Towers* and very soon he appears in BBC1's *Lingo* – a programme all about learning languages.

THERE'S NO NEED TO LEARN A FOREIGN LANGUAGE — JUST SHOUT A LITTLE LOUDER IN ENGLISH.

You remember that's what Basil Fawlty thought, when he tried to make his Spanish waiter, Manuel, understand him.

But then Basil was a rude, ignorant sort of chap, wasn't he? Quite different, of course, from your typical British businessman or woman.

Unfortunately, British businesspeople are rather arrogant about learning foreign languages. Or rather, <u>not</u> learning them.

Unlike their European competitors, who set aside 5% of management time for foreign language training. Unlike the employees of a famous German car maker who go to language lessons every week. (Outside company time, that is.)

Of course, maybe that's the point. You don't have to learn a foreign language because everyone else in Europe can speak English.

Wrong. They can't.

Which means that if you can't make yourself understood in your customer's language, you risk losing sales.

Reason enough, surely, to make language training a vital part of your Single Market business plan. However busy you are.

After all, as Manuel would say: *En el Mercado Unico todo el mundo habla varios idiomas.*

Annoying, isn't it?

The Polytechnic of South Essex. Language Courses for businesspeople. Ring us: 0720–58763

6
Work in a group. Why is there a need for advertisements such as the one above or programmes such as *Lingo*?

7
Read the factfile. How does language teaching in your country's schools compare with that in British schools?

8
Write a short article about language learning in your country. Don't forget to give it a title.

Factfile | Languages

1
Most British schoolchildren begin studying a foreign language when they enter secondary school at the age of 11.

2
Under the reformed educational system, the National Curriculum, *all* British schoolchildren must learn one modern foreign language between the ages of 11 and 16.

3
Until the National Curriculum was introduced nearly 60% of students opted out of their foreign language classes at the age of 14.

4
In the GCSE exam which students take at age 16, candidates are expected to be able to speak and write in a manner which would be understood by a native speaker, on a range of topics.

5
The most popular foreign language is French, although German, Spanish, and Italian are also studied.

6
There are shortages of teachers in all languages. A further 3,000 teachers of modern languages will be needed if plans to encourage language learning go ahead.

Section B

1

Read through the extracts and find out which person . . . .

a is in favour of a single European currency
b feels truly European
c thinks the standard of living in Britain is lower than in France
d is excited about the new vision of Europe
e wants each country in Europe to keep its own identity

2

Match these titles with the extracts.
We can link up in a spirit of peace.
Brussels could teach us a lot.

3

Work in pairs and summarise the views of the two writers.

4

Consider in your pairs the question you answered in Section A, activity **1**: *How European are the British?* Have your views changed?

5

Imagine in your pairs that you are a foreigner living in your country. What is life like for you? How do you find the people and the cost of living? How do you feel? Write a paragraph.

Suzi Stembridge, 50, has always worked in travel. She and her husband own a holiday consultancy firm, *Grecofile*.

"MY FIRST job was in a travel agency. Later, I worked as an air-stewardess and when my children came along I did some travel writing. Five years ago I started *Grecofile*, to give an unbiased service that offers people the holiday they really want.

I fell in love with Greece the moment I landed at Athens for the first time. I remember thinking, this was *exactly* what I was looking for.

I think I've always felt European but I don't want to see us all becoming standardised.

I'd like to keep our identity and our separate currency; I like the fact that we have different languages and even, in the case of the Greeks, a different alphabet. I love the various European styles of food and cooking and definitely don't want everything to have a common international flavour.

I find it challenging and exciting, this vision of Europe: it's very much in a spirit of peace that we can link up like this, and I think it's a wonderful thing."

Roy Clementson, 59, has been a long-distance lorry driver for more than 30 years, and recently won a diploma of honour for 20 years' accident-free driving.

"I PREFER driving in Europe because there are better facilities. It's easier to get a shower and there are far more decent places to eat, especially in France.

I'm not one of those drivers who won't eat anything except sausage, eggs, beans and chips. I like French food and I like the prices they charge. In France, if you look around, you can get a five-course meal and as much wine as you can drink for £5.50. In Italy the food is very good, but it is expensive: more like £10 per meal.

I can assure you all the drivers would welcome a single European currency. It would be much better if you didn't have to change money all the time. I've got nothing against the Royal Family, but not having coins with the Queen's picture on doesn't make any difference to me.

I don't see any disadvantages in going into Europe. I think the French and Germans have a better standard of living than we do. I recently saw a beautiful four-bedroomed house that cost about £75,000 in France. Now, my house is worth more than that, but it's only about one-third the size.

People talk about our being ruled by Brussels; well, I think we could pick up a lot of good ideas. I wouldn't say I *feel* European, but I don't agree with people who have this attitude that we're somehow better than they are. We have a lot to learn."

Section C

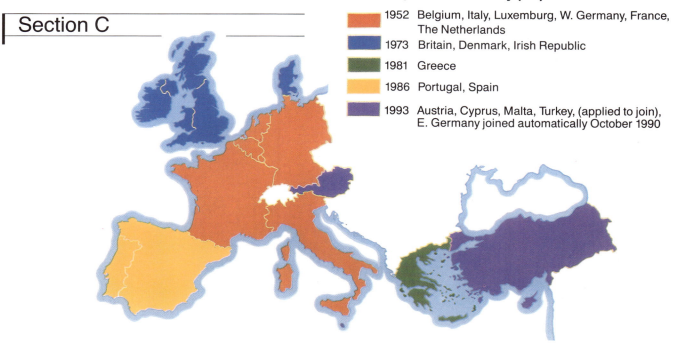

The European Community (EC)

■ (orange)	1952	Belgium, Italy, Luxemburg, W. Germany, France, The Netherlands
■ (blue)	1973	Britain, Denmark, Irish Republic
■ (green)	1981	Greece
■ (yellow)	1986	Portugal, Spain
■ (purple)	1993	Austria, Cyprus, Malta, Turkey, (applied to join), E. Germany joined automatically October 1990

Who the UK send to the European Community

UK MEP's
32 Conservative
45 Labour
 1 Scottish Nationalist
 1 Ulster Unionist
 1 Social Democratic
  & Labour party

The Council of Ministers in Brussels makes the major policy decisions of the EC. It is formed of government ministers from member states.

The UK nominates two commissioners to the European Commission.

There are 12 members of the court of Auditors, based in Luxemburg which supervises how the budget is managed.

The Court of Justice sits in Luxemburg and comprises 13 judges.

The Economic and Social Committee meets in Brussels. It is a consultative body with 189 members, 24 of these from the UK.

The European Parliament in Strasbourg has 518 representatives or MEP's. 81 of them are from the UK.

Project

Work in a group to prepare a **Britain and Europe** factfile.
a Look at the information on the map and diagram and select the most relevant facts to include in your factfile.
b Include facts from the rest of the unit if you like.

c Research further information in books, magazines and newspapers.
d Prepare your factfile.
e Display it on the classroom walls for the rest of the class to read.

'What are you reading?'

Books can change your life. But do people in Britain still read books or has television killed off the reading habit? And, speaking of killing, what is a sweet 70 year-old grandmother doing writing best-selling stories of violent murder?

Section A

1

Answer these questions.

a What newspapers do you read?
b What magazines do you read?
c How many books do you read in your free time in a year?
d Are you reading a book at the moment?

2

Use the information in the factfile to complete the newspaper article.

3

Work in a group. Discuss the information in the newspaper article and the factfile. Does anything surprise you? Why?

Reading remains popular despite television

BOOKS AND the pleasures of reading have not been eclipsed by television. The average home has _____ books and one in ten families has more than 500, according to a study of consumer attitudes.

_____ thirds of households have a Bible and a _____ and 56 per cent of adults have a library ticket. Regular readers show a distinct liking for puzzle and quiz books.

The survey of 900 adults shows that four in five had bought at least one book in the past _____ months and that giving books as presents was popular.

Two-fifths of all books purchased are bought for others as _____ or birthday presents and 41 per cent had also bought a book for a _____ in the past year. The research was commissioned because publishers feared books were in long-term decline.

Regular readers estimated that they spent an average 7.8 hours a week reading.

Women are the most enthusiastic readers, spending _____ hours a week reading, compared with _____ hours for men.

The most popular books are _____ stories, thrillers and (for women) romance. But about _____ of regular readers tackle a work of non-fiction regularly.

Factfile | Reading

1
The average British home has 200 books. One family in ten have more than 500 books.

2
Sixty-six per cent of households have a dictionary and The Bible.

3
In a recent survey 59% of people said they had read a book in the last month. Eighty per cent of adults said they had bought a book in the last twelve months.

4
Forty per cent of all books bought in Britain are bought for other people, as Christmas or birthday presents.

5
Forty-one per cent of people interviewed said they had bought a book for a child in the last twelve months.

6
Regular readers estimated that they spent an average of 7.8 hours a week reading books. Women spend more time reading books than men (8.6 hours compared with 6.7 hours).

7
The most popular kinds of books are crime stories, thrillers, and romance. But 75% of regular readers also read non-fiction.

8
There are free public libraries throughout Britain. In 1991 British public libraries held 137 million books in stock and issued more than 600 million books a year.

9
Fifty-six per cent of people hold a current public library ticket.

10
The British Library in London has a stock of over 18 million items. Publishers must give the British Library a copy of every book they publish.

Section B

1

a How many of these words and expressions do you know?

1 exports	4 transferred
2 dramatically	5 a deal
3 as a result	6 recouped

b Match the words with the synonyms below.
an agreement   consequently   recovered
overseas sales   spectacularly   moved

c Now read the article below and find the words and expressions in activity **1a**.

2

Work with a partner. Find evidence in the article that supports the statements below.

a Books are big business.
b Yet by the beginning of 1991 the British book trade was in trouble.
c But there were other problems apart from sales.

3

Use the information in the boxes below to complete this paragraph.

Sally Beauman received £340,000 for *Destiny* – more than .... times what P D James got for *Devices and Desires*. .... *Devices and Desires* sold more than .... as many hardback copies as *Destiny*. The paperback sales of the two books were very similar. Yet .... of the large advance paid for *Destiny* and the £75,000 spent on ...., *Destiny* actually lost £160,000. *Devices and Desires*, on the other ...., made a substantial .... for its publishers.

Books are big business. In 1989 British publishers produced 62,000 books. Many of these books were sold outside Britain. In the same year the value of British book exports was over £660 million.

Yet by the beginning of 1991 the British book trade was in trouble. Sales were down dramatically. As a result, many people working in publishing lost their jobs – 250 in a single week in March 1991.

But there were other problems apart from sales. One of the most important was the huge increase in the sums of money publishers were willing to pay in order to capture famous authors. Big names like Jeffrey Archer and Ken Follett transferred from one publisher to another for millions of pounds, just like football stars. In July 1990 Archer signed a deal to write three books for the publishers Harper Collins at a price of £11 million. In the same month Follett signed a similar deal with Dell for £7 million.

There seemed to be little chance of these huge sums being recouped from sales. Thus, many publishers lost a good deal of money on books from star authors which the public refused to buy in sufficient quantities. If you pay an author a six-figure sum to write a book, you've got to sell an awful lot of copies to make a profit on it, or even to get your money back.

THE PROFIT

PD James
Devices and Desires

Advance:
£100,000

Hardback Sales:
160,000

Paperbacks:
645,000

Approx earnings:
£450,000

Approx profit:
£350,000

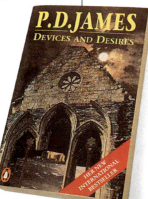

THE LOSSES

Sally Beauman
Destiny

Advance:
£340,000
+ £75,000 promotion

Hardback Sales:
75,000

Paperbacks:
600,000

Approx earnings:
£255,000

Approx loss:
£160,000

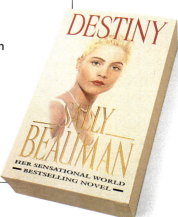

Section C

1

Read the article and complete the chart with important dates in the life of P D James.

event	date
born	1921
first job	....
married	....
first book	....
husband died	....

P(hyllis) D(orothy) James is one of Britain's leading writers. She has not always been a writer. Indeed, for many years she had a job, two children, and an invalid husband. Life was difficult.

Much of Phyllis James's life is a tale of triumph over adversity. Childhood in the Twenties was overshadowed by the First World War; education in the Thirties at Cambridge Girls' High School was good but too short.

She still minds that her parents had neither money nor desire to send a daughter to university. At 16 she started to work for the Inland Revenue (as her father did) and then married a medical student, Connor Bantry White, in 1941. They had two daughters, Jane and Claire, but he came back from the war suffering from schizophrenia and was in and out of hospital for the rest of his life. (He died in 1964.)

They moved in with Connor's parents in Essex in 1950 and Phyllis, aged 29, found a job keeping medical records. She attended evening classes at the City of London College before taking a diploma at the Institute of Hospital Administrators. At the same time she

began to work on her first novel, which was published in 1962. "So I was getting up at six to write, wrote more in the train on the way to work, then there were evening classes before going home . . . my husband was ill . . . it was not easy."

2

P D James was asked these questions in an interview. Read the questions. What kind of novels does she write?

a When you were a child, did you think about death more than other children?
b Did you have a happy childhood?
c Did you feel secure?
d Were you aware – growing up – of violent crime?
e Have you ever personally come into contact with murder?
f Why did you choose to write crime fiction?

3

a Work with a partner. What do you think P D James's replies to the six questions might have been?
b Now read her replies below. Match them to the questions in **2**
c How accurate were your predictions?

1 "No. I never felt secure. Never."

2 "I didn't want to write about the things that have happened to me in my own life – I never have really – and I love the craft of the detective novel. You really have to construct it."

3 "No. No, I never have really. Of course I lived through a war. There was plenty of death but we never saw it . . ."

4 "Mmmmm . . . fairly happy. I was happy at school. Parts of it were very happy. I grew up in beautiful places."

5 "No. No. I never knew of it when I was young. And in fact the years before the Second World War were very peaceful, in terms of crime rates, astonishingly so. It's hard to say why.

6 "No. No. I don't think so. Although I was always fascinated by it . . . I think I really was quite powerfully influenced by being born two years after the end of the '14-18' War. My father had been a machine-gun officer. My mother would speak of boys who had gone to war, never come back . . ."

4

In one of P D James's most popular books Cordelia Gray is investigating Mark Callendar's death. She is staying in the cottage in the country that Mark lived in. She goes up to London to look for some evidence, then returns to the cottage. Now read on . . .

She caught the eighteen-sixteen train from Liverpool Street and it was nearly eight o'clock before she arrived back at the cottage. She parked the Mini in its usual place in the shelter of the copse and made her way round the side of the cottage. She hesitated for a moment wondering whether to collect the gun from its hiding place but decided that this could wait until later. She was hungry and the first priority was to get a meal. She had carefully locked the back door and had stuck a thin strip of Scotch tape across the window sill before leaving that morning. If there were any more secret visitors she wanted to be warned. But the tape was still intact. She felt in her shoulder bag for the key and, bending down, fitted it into the lock.

a What precautions had Cordelia taken before leaving the cottage?
b What had she been expecting?

She wasn't expecting trouble outside the cottage and the attack took her completely by surprise. There was the half-second of pre-knowledge before the blanket fell but that was too late. There was a cord around her neck pulling the mask of hot stifling wool taut against her mouth and nostrils. She gasped for breath and tasted the dry strong-smelling fibres on her tongue. Then a sharp pain exploded in her chest and she remembered nothing.

c What do you think caused the *sharp pain*?

The movement of liberation was a miracle and a horror. The blanket was whipped off. She never saw her assailant. There was a second of sweet reviving air, a glimpse, so brief that it was barely comprehended, of blinding sky seen through greenness and then she felt herself falling, falling in helpless astonishment into cold darkness. The fall was a confusion of old nightmares, unbelievable seconds of childhood terrors recalled. Then her body hit the water. Ice-cold hands dragged her into a vortex of horror. Instinctively, she had closed her mouth at the moment of impact and she struggled to the surface through what seemed an eternity of cold encompassing blackness. She shook her head and, through her stinging eyes, she looked up. The black tunnel that stretched above her ended in a moon of blue light. Even as she looked, the well lid was dragged slowly back like the shutter of a camera. The moon became a half moon; then a crescent. At last there was nothing but eight thin slits of light.

d Where is Cordelia?

Desperately she trod water, reaching tentatively for the bottom. There was no bottom. Frantically moving hands and feet, willing herself not to panic, she felt around the walls of the well for a possible foothold. There was none. The funnel of bricks, smooth, sweating with moisture, stretched around and above her like a circular tomb. As she gazed upwards they writhed, expanded, swayed and reeled like the belly of a monstrous snake.

And then she felt a saving anger. She wouldn't let her-self drown, wouldn't die in this horrible place, alone and terrified. The well was deep but small, the diameter barely three feet. If she kept her head and took time, she could brace her legs and shoulders against the bricks and work her way upwards.

She hadn't bruised or stunned herself against the walls as she fell. Miraculously she was uninjured. The fall had been clean. She was alive and capable of thought. She had always been a survivor. She would survive.

e How do you think Cordelia is going to try to get out of the well?
f What do you think will happen when she gets to the top of the well?

5

Work with a partner. Read the extract again.

a At what points does Cordelia feel these emotions?
   1 determination 2 anger 3 panic

b How would you have felt in Cordelia's situation?

Section D

Billy is a murderer. At the age of 18 he killed a man and was sentenced to life imprisonment. While inside he decided he wanted to change: he wanted to get an education. He asked his friends to send him books. There was one book that seemed to speak to him particularly, a book of poems. The book was *Four Quartets* by T S Eliot. Billy describes what happened when he tried to read it.

When I first tried to read it, I couldn't make head nor tail of it; and I couldn't the second or even the twenty-second time either. But then suddenly one day it was like somebody had switched a blinding light on, and it all started to have a lot of meaning. I'd never read anything like it before in my whole life: it wasn't so much like he was talking to you as he was putting his own thoughts down on paper and letting you see them as they passed through his mind.

I read it and read it and read it, and there were great huge chunks of it I could say off by heart. Not because I ever sat down and learnt them because I didn't, but because they kept floating into my mind in the same way I imagine they did into his. I still remember how '*Burnt Norton*' starts off:

> Time present and time past
> Are both perhaps present in
>   time future,
> And time future contained in
>   time past.
> If all time is eternally present
> All time is unredeemable.

and like I say, you have to read it 20 times before you understand it; but then once you do, you follow his train of thought from there.

I'd been lucky, they'd been fairly lenient with me and I'd only had to do nine years which was about average, and that was the end of that and I was going to start again from there. It's true to say without any argument at all that I came out better than I'd gone in: definitely as far as education was concerned, and with at least some improvement in personality too. It's terrible it had to be at the cost of someone else's life though, that has to be said. It's something I can't undo, but it should never have happened; if they'd kept me in for good it wouldn't have been any more than I deserved, I'm well aware of that.

1

a Read the introduction to the article only.

b Before you read more about Billy, discuss with a partner how reading something might change your life.

2

Read the article. Find the words and expressions which mean the following:

a not understand (parag. 1)

b by memory (parag. 2)

c way of thinking (parag. 2)

d without doubt (parag. 3)

3

Work with a partner.

a Which word do you think best describes how Billy felt when he came out of prison?

  1 angry   2 sorry   3 fortunate

b What do you think of his attitude to his crime and the punishment he received?

4

With your partner, write a short summary of Billy's experiences.

5

Think of a book which has had an effect on you. Write a paragraph saying *how* it affected you.

Project

Work in a group to draw up a list of books in your language that would be suitable for people who are learning your language.

Think about these questions:

a *What age are your learners?*

b *What language level are they – beginner, intermediate, advanced?*

c *What kind of books will you include – fiction or non-fiction? (If fiction, what kind – serious novels, detective stories, science fiction, romance? If non-fiction – biography, psychology, history?)*

Does accent matter?

What is a dialect? What is an accent? Is the way you speak in Britain sometimes more important than what you say? What influences have made English the language it is today?

Section A

1

a Answer these questions about your attitude to language.

1 Do you speak differently at home to how you speak at school or work?
2 Do you speak differently on the telephone?
3 Do you like the way you speak?
4 Has the way you speak been affected by where you live?
5 Have you ever made fun of the way somebody else speaks?
6 Has anyone ever made fun of the way you speak?
7 Have you ever been put off someone by the way he/she speaks?
8 Do you speak the same way as your parents?

b Work with a partner. Compare your answers.

2

Look at the photograph showing the two women. What do you think they are doing?

3

Now read the article. Why is Paula Gower changing the way she speaks?

It ain't what you say...

...it's *still* the way you say it.
Rosalind Sharpe on the new interest in 'talking proper'.

Tongue twisters: *Lucie Clayton* student **Paula Gower (right)** demonstrates 'vocal aerobics'; **Odette Lawley (left)** says: "Release the jaw to free the sound".

PAULA GOWER has a four-star accent, but it is unobtrusive. Over the phone, her voice is soft and tuneful with a regional inflection (she comes from a village just outside Norwich). She sounds attentive and sensible. It is a surprise to discover that she is only 23.

The Sprowston Manor Hotel, where Ms Gower is deputy manager, has recently been improved to four star standard. Ms Gower's new voice is part of this refurbishment: the hotel's owner, Tim Spurrier, sent her on a two-day course at the Lucie Clayton School in London to learn "voice and communication" along with corporate dress sense and business make-up.

For the voice part of the course, she had to listen to a recording of herself reading a passage from a book. The voice teacher, Odette Lawley, diagnosed that Ms Gower was speaking too quickly and biting the ends off her words. She taught her to breath correctly, slow down and modify her Norfolk vowels slightly. At the end of the course, they re-recorded the same passage. "You wouldn't have thought it was the same person," said Ms Gower.

"It gave her confidence," said Mr Spurrier, who paid £390 plus VAT for the course. "Now she looks people in the face. Before she had a tendency to look at her feet."

4

Match each of the following sentences with the paragraph it summarises.

a Paula Gower was sent on a voice-improvement course by the Hotel's owner.
b She was taught to slow her speech and change her accent slightly.
c She has gained confidence.
d Paula has a pleasant voice and sounds older than she is.

5

Choose the best synonym for each of these words in the article:

a *four-star*
   good   excellent   fair
b *refurbishment*
   improvement   rebuilding   refurnishing
c *diagnosed*
   realised   discovered   was surprised

6

Now read the rest of the article from the previous page. Who is John Honey? What is the title of his book?

Dr Honey, socio-linguist and teacher of English at Kumamoto University, Japan, and author of *Does Accent Matter?*, boldly uses the word 'class' when he talks about accent. In his book he describes research in which people are played tapes of the same messages being read in various ways, then asked to award attributes to the voices they have heard.

The stereotypes are consistently confirmed: people ascribe competence, efficiency and even (ludicrously) cleanliness and good looks to voices which speak in 'Received Pronunciation'. Speakers of RP are thought likely to be lawyers and bank managers.

Regional accents persistently fall into a hierarchy with Yorkshire, West Country and, anomalously, Geordie (Newcastle) near the top. Lodged at the bottom are the five accents of the working-class industrial cities – Cockney (London), Liverpool, Birmingham, Glasgow and Belfast. People still imagine the owners of these accents to be manual workers; on television these are the accents of comics and villains.

John Honey has no scruples about telling people they should jettison their working-class accents: he thinks they are a huge barrier to progress towards equality. "We have to choose between the museum approach, which keeps these accents on in glass cases even though they are rotting the chances of the people who use them, or we recognise that the world would be a drearier but a fairer place if we got rid of them."

And how we do that? In schools, of course, where much more attention should be paid to English language – grammar and spelling as well as clear, intelligible speech. But to Dr Honey's disappointment, the new National Curriculum contains no requirement to teach Received Pronunciation. Brian Cox, who advised the Government on its development, sympathises with Honey's ideas but says they are impracticable. Consequently, the curriculum requires only that children be taught "to speak Standard English in an accent which is clear and comprehensible".

7

Work with a partner.

a Which of these points are mentioned in the article?

1 Dr Honey recorded different people reading the same message.
2 Listeners rated Received Pronunciation speakers more highly than other speakers.
3 Dr Honey explains why accents like Cockney have low status.
4 Dr Honey thinks that people should drop working-class accents.

b Choose the three most important points made in the article.

8

Continue working with your partner. How do you feel about the way you speak your own language? Is there anything you would like to change?

9

Read the factfile. Does anything surprise you? Write a factfile about accents in your country.

F*actfile* | Accents

1
Only about 3% of the British population speak RP.

2
The new National Curriculum for schools contains no requirement to teach RP. It requires only that children are taught 'to speak in an accent which is clear and comprehensible'.

3
Accents seem to have greater power to affect an individual's life in Britain than in many other comparable countries.

4
In the 1930's many schools taught elocution but since the 1960's any mention of accent has been taboo in state schools.

5
The very posh form of RP traditionally spoken by the Royal Family is nowadays widely downgraded.

6
The BBC's RP ranks at the top of the accent hierarchy with popular London speech at the bottom.

Section B

1

Read the short text below. Why does the author say that *English is a very mixed-up language*?

English is a very mixed-up language. Its grammar is similar to German, but its vocabulary is drawn from French, Latin, German, and a host of other languages. For example, in the sentence:

He smuggled a beef sandwich into the dormitory in his anorak.

smuggled is a Dutch word, *beef* comes from French, *sandwich* is named after the man who invented it, *dormitory* is from Latin, and *anorak* is an Eskimo word!

How did this mixed-up language become the way it is today?

2

Read the *first* part of the article below, *The dawn of English*. Name three invaders and find the years in which they arrived in Britain.

3

Read the *second* part of the article, *1066 and all that*. Who spoke French? Why? Which new language was formed?

4

Read the *third* part, *Hot off the press*.

a What was Caxton's big problem?
b How did the invention of printing affect the English language?

5

Read the *final* part, *Now here is the news from the BBC*.

a Find five new expressions.
b Can you think of any other new words which describe fashions or inventions?

The dawn of English
500BC–AD1066

About 2,500 years ago a tribe called the Celts arrived in the British Isles. They came from Europe and spoke a language we now call Celtic.

By the time the Romans invaded in 55BC a number of Celtic languages had developed. For the next 500 years the Romans tried hard to take over the country and its language.

The Romans spoke Latin. They built camps in various parts of Britain. A great many Latin words found their way into the English language, either at this time or later. The word *Englaland*, later shortened to *England*, started to be used in about AD1000. By now several new groups of people had invaded. The best-known of the invaders were the Angles and the Saxons who landed in AD700. We call the language which they spoke Anglo-Saxon or Old English.

1066 and all that
AD1066–AD1400

In AD1066 the Normans invaded. They came from Normandy in France and brought their language with them. Although ordinary people continued to use English, the up-and-coming middle classes all adopted French as their language. To get on in society it became essential to speak French. As a result of this a new language began to be formed. Slowly Old English and French merged together into something which we now call Middle English.

Hot off the press
AD1400–AD1800

The next big change came about because of an invention – the printing press. In 1476 William Caxton started printing books in London. But he faced a major problem. People who lived in different parts of the country spoke English in their own different ways. They used different words to describe the same things and the way those words were put together in a sentence depended on what part of the country they were in.

When Caxton came to print what people said or wrote he had to choose his words and decide how to spell them. He took the easy way out: he nearly always chose his own dialect, the dialect of London and the East Midlands.

The increase in the number of printed books and pamphlets meant that gradually spelling was becoming standardised.

Now here is the news from the BBC
AD1800–the present day

In the last two centuries technology has really left its mark on our language. Newspapers, mass-produced books, libraries, films, radio and finally television have all played their part. New words have come into the language from all over the world. Words such as *radar or laser* have been invented to describe new inventions. Fashions have come and gone at great speed leaving such words as *punk, heavy metal, house music* or *rave* behind them.

Section C

1

a Answer these questions.

1 What is the national language of your country?
2 Are any other languages spoken in your country?
3 Do you speak any of them?

b Work in a group. Discuss your answers.

2

English is not the only language spoken in Britain. In England, there are thousands of native speakers of Urdu, Bengali, and Hindi in cities such as Bradford, Birmingham, and London. In other parts of Britain, languages other than English are also spoken. In Wales 19% of the population speak Welsh, a Celtic language; in Scotland, 2% of the population speak Gaelic, another Celtic language.

Read through the article on the right until you find out which language the article is about.

3

Read the first three paragraphs. Match these synonyms with the words underlined in the passage.

a banned   d strongholds
b remains   e lost its strength
c mass   f invented

4

Read the three paragraphs again and complete the table with brief notes on the differences between the past (**then**) and the present (**now**).

	then	now
Celtic culture		
Gaelic language		
Skye		

5

Why is the article entitled *The Last of the Gaels*?

6

Work with a partner. How do you think people on Skye might feel about the decline in Gaelic? Do you think . . . ?

a they are proud of their language and want to preserve it
b they think Gaelic is of little use in the modern world
c they think it's more useful to learn English
d they think it's a pity that Gaelic is declining, but it can't be helped

7

Read the last four paragraphs. What do three Skye residents say about Gaelic? Which of the above feelings does each of them agree with?

Project

Write an article about a language that was once widely spoken but has now died out or almost died out. Think about these questions:
Who speaks/spoke the language?
Where do/did they live?
Is/was the language encouraged or discouraged?

Last Day of the Gaels

Six small children sit in a school corridor in Broadford on the Isle of Skye reading and chatting in Gaelic. They are the last of a dying tribe, the northern <u>remnant</u> of what was once a glorious Celtic culture stretching far across the European continent. In their time the Celts produced fine ballads and outstanding art, keeping the light of Christian culture burning while the rest of Britain <u>languished</u> in the Dark Ages.

Now the Gaelic children of Skye are reading translations of *Biff and Chip's Birthday Party* and *Pip and the Little Monkey* in their native tongue. The teaching materials are all <u>improvised</u>. Only a few years ago the Gaelic language was <u>proscribed</u> in school and it is not long since any child who spoke it in the classroom was severely beaten. Only 473 Scots children under five still speak Gaelic according to the last census, in 1981.

Yet Skye was once thought of as the heart of the *Gaeltachd*, the land of the Gaels. The only large <u>concentration</u> of Gaelic-speakers still left on the island live on the north-east tip, the Staffin peninsula. This parish is one of the last <u>redoubts</u> of the northern Gaels. All around the Gaelic culture may be dying, but in Staffin the traditional community survives.

Mairi Ross, who lives in Staffin, commutes daily to Portree to work in the Caledonian Café. According to her, all the children in Staffin know Gaelic but seldom use it now. They dropped it when they went to school in Portree. At the Portree high school the other children teased the Gaelic speakers, calling them *teuchtars* – that is, bumpkins (uneducated people of the land).

"It doesn't bother me," says Mairi, "but some of the other Staffin kids get very upset. I now feel comfier speaking in English. Gaelic will probably die out. It's a shame but people just aren't bothering.

The older crofters are little more enthusiastic. "It's a good language," says John Mackenzie, a crofter whose brother runs the village shop in Staffin. "But I'm not sure it's a hundred per cent necessary. And the young people are not very keen: the newcomers seem far more interested than the locals."

"The Gaelic pressure groups are full of London newcomers," said one of the teachers at Broadford. "They stick a tuft of heather in each ear, dress up in kilts and start learning Gaelic. But the young people here aren't interested. Gaelic is presented as something that's one million years old. They think it doesn't get you anywhere; you just stay on your croft and stay poor. As far as they're concerned, it's better to learn English and head south."

Class struggle

Britain's schools have been through some changes. A new National Curriculum has been introduced. How do the teachers feel about all the extra responsibilities? What are the options available to 16 year olds in the 1990's?

Section A

1

What do you know about British education? How many of the questions in the factfile can you answer?

2

Work with a partner.

a Discuss your answers.
b Check your answers on page 87.
c Do any of these facts surprise you?

Factfile | Education

1

In Britain you have to attend school between . . . .

a 5 and 16
b 5 and 18
c 7 and 16

2

A comprehensive school is . . . .

a a school of languages
b a school for 5–11 year olds
c a school for 11–16 year olds

3

'Public' schools like Eton in the photograph are very expensive – it costs more than £10,000 a year to be educated at Eton, for example.

What proportion of British children attend 'public' schools?

a 7%
b 10%
c 15%

4

In 1989 a new National Curriculum was introduced into British schools. Ten subjects had to be studed. Three of these subjects (called *Core Subjects*) were chosen for special attention.

Here are the ten subjects to be studied. Which do you think are the *Core Subjects*?

a English
b History
c Geography
d Art
e Science
f Mathematics
g a foreign language
h Design and Technology
i Physical Education
j Music

5

16 year olds in Britain have to take General Certificate of Secondary Education examinations. Girls have significantly better results than boys in three of the following GCSE subjects. Which three?

a Mathematics
b English
c Biology
d History
e French
f Chemistry

6

The average pupil-teacher ratio in British schools is . . . .

a 19
b 22
c 25
d 30

7

A grammar school is . . . .

a a school for 11–18 year olds who have all passed an entrance examination
b a school where learning languages is important
c a school for the children of wealthy families

Section B

1

Read these headlines and short extracts. Who is complaining here? What are their complaints?

Pupils sent home as teachers join strike

A TEACHERS' strike yesterday closed schools in Britain and affected an estimated 2 million children.

Teachers 'wilting' under paperwork

TEACHERS ARE too over-burdened by administration to carry out all the classroom tests in the National Curriculum.

2

Work with a partner. Look at the information in the table. Discuss the figures.

a What conclusion do you draw from them?
b What questions would you like to ask about them?

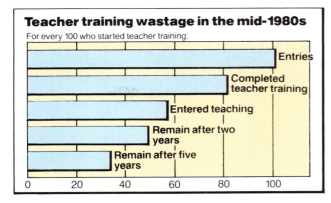

Teacher training wastage in the mid-1980s

For every 100 who started teacher training:

- Entries
- Completed teacher training
- Entered teaching
- Remain after two years
- Remain after five years

0   20   40   60   80   100

3

Read the first three paragraphs of the article about a British schoolteacher and say which paragraphs describe . . . .

a Lesley Crouch's standard of living
b what she teaches
c her qualifications and training

Pace of change sows the seeds of disillusion

LESLEY CROUCH, 31, has been a teacher in Leeds for 10 years. She earns £16,898 a year before tax and is nearly at the top of her professional salary scale. She owns a one-bedroom flat, runs a four year-old Ford Fiesta car and most of her holidays are trips abroad with the school orchestra.

She teaches drama, but began as a music teacher. Now she also offers General Studies and Life Skills at her 13 to 18 high school in Leeds.

After grammar school and a music degree from Leeds University she took a one-year teacher training course and went to teach at the school where she has remained all her teaching career.

She can rise to one more point on the salary scale and then: "I stop. I have to move school, find another job if I want to move up." She can only get more money is she is promoted. "But I like what I am doing here, I like the kids and my colleagues and that is important. But you have to move if you want to get on."

All the higher allowances for teachers are, she says, for administration or added responsibility and any school has only so many to hand out.

Pay is not her main worry: "It is not pay that is the damaging thing. What I am disillusioned and bitter about is the speed at which changes have been introduced. It makes the job so difficult. It is a shame to be in a profession where I have to weigh my self-interest against the good of the kids."

4

Read the rest of the article. Are these statements about Lesley true or false?

a She started teaching when she was 21.
b She wants to become an administrator.
c She teaches the subject she studied at university.
d She is involved in music at her school.
e She doesn't like her school.
f She is more worried about pay than anything else.

5

Work in groups. How do teachers feel about their profession in your country? Do they have similar problems to teachers in Britain? If so, what should be done to improve the situation?

Section C

1

Read the paragraph below and complete this simple flowchart showing the options available to young people after GCSE's.

GCSE passes
↓
....
↙   ↘
....

Most pupils take their GCSE exams when they're 16. Those who get good grades can stay on at school for a further two years and sit their A-level exams. Good A-level results make it possible for pupils to go on to further education in a university or polytechnic.

2

Now look at the flowchart on the right. What choices do you have if you . . . ?

a don't get good GCSE grades

b get good grades but don't want to do A-levels

c get good grades, want to do A-levels, but don't want to stay at school

3

Imagine that you are a British student. You've got good GSCE grades and want to do A-levels. Which educational institution would you choose to do them in? Why?

4

Work with a partner. Choose a situation from the flow-chart. Role-play an interview between a Careers Adviser and a student in that situation.

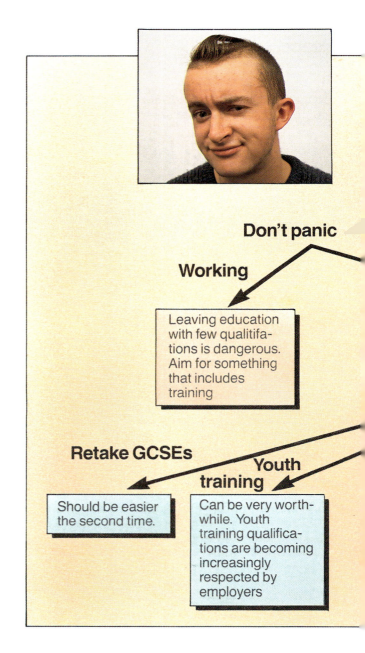

Don't panic

Working

Leaving education with few qualitifations is dangerous. Aim for something that includes training

Retake GCSEs

Should be easier the second time.

Youth training

Can be very worthwhile. Youth training qualifications are becoming increasingly respected by employers

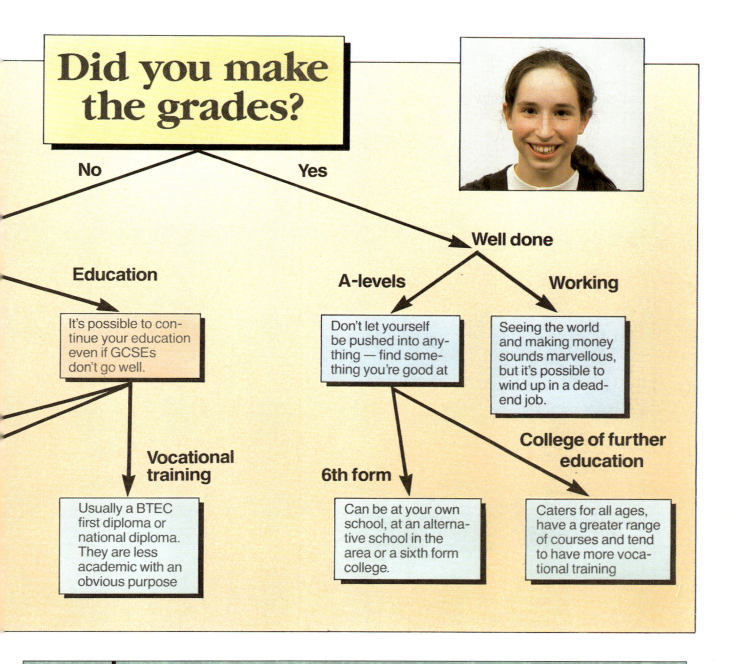

Did you make the grades?

No   **Yes**

Well done

Education

It's possible to continue your education even if GCSEs don't go well.

A-levels

Don't let yourself be pushed into anything — find something you're good at

Working

Seeing the world and making money sounds marvellous, but it's possible to wind up in a dead-end job.

College of further education

Vocational training

Usually a BTEC first diploma or national diploma. They are less academic with an obvious purpose

6th form

Can be at your own school, at an alternative school in the area or a sixth form college.

Caters for all ages, have a greater range of courses and tend to have more vocational training

---

Project

Work in groups. Design a flow-chart showing the options available to school-leavers in your country.

Points you need to think about when you are designing your chart include:

- at what age can you leave school?
- what school-leaving examinations can you take?

- what opportunities are there if you fail these examinations?
- what training opportunities are there?
- what organisations help school-leavers to find jobs?
- what organisations help school-leavers to find places on training schemes?

Working for a living

What do people in Britain expect from a job? Money, yes – but what else? How do young people feel about starting work? Why do some people prefer to set up on their own?

Section A

1
Complete the factfile with the figures given below.

- 27.1 million
- 11.3%   43%
- £4,524
- 29.8 hours   43.5 hours
- 1935   1990

2
Work with a partner.

a Discuss your figures.
b Check your answers on page 88.
c Do any of these facts surprise you?

3
In groups read the factfile again and write captions for the two photographs.

Factfile | Employment

1
In 1990 the number of British people in full-time work was .... , the highest number ever.

2
Between 1979 and 1989 the number of self-employed people rose by 70% to 3.2 million. This equalled .... of the total workforce.

3
In 1992 the highest-paid man in Britain was the managing director of a bank. He received an annual salary of £1,339,000. In the same year a kitchen porter in a British Hospital, received an annual salary of ....

4
In 1971 women made up 37% of the labour force in Britain. By 1988 this had risen to ....

5
On average British men work longer hours than men in other European countries (..................... per week as opposed to 40.7)

6
On average women work fewer hours than their European sisters (..................... as opposed to 33.4).

7
In 1990 fewer than 200,000 working days were lost through strike action. This is the lowest figure since ....

8
Trade unions lost 25% of their members between 1980 and ....

9
The Youth Training Scheme (YTS) was introduced in 1983. It offered two years of training for 16-year old school leavers.

Section B

1

Look at the table below. They show the results of a survey amongst British teenagers. Which of these words and expressions would you use to describe their attitudes?

adventurous   conservative   family-oriented
home-loving   materialistic   ambitious

Which factors are most important in a job?		
Factor	**Male %**	**Female %**
Job satisfaction	58	66
Money	29	13
Friendly atmosphere	7	13
Good conditions	5	6
Training	3	3
Travel	1	2

Where they would like to work		
Location	**Male %**	**Female %**
In home area	50	43
Elsewhere in UK	30	37
In London	14	16
Abroad	36	40

The survey sought the views of almost 1,500 16-18 year-olds studying at schools and colleges throughout Britain. It shows that most teenagers have fairly traditional ambitions. They are most likely to want to stay in their home region and build a secure future. Those that want to work abroad see it as a short-term investment in good experience for later careers at home.

2

Work in a group. What do/would you look for in a job? Discuss your views. Are your attitudes similar to or different from the views of the British teenagers in the survey?

3

Read the article *In their words* and discuss these questions with a partner.

a How many people were interviewed for the article?
b How old are they?
c What have they just done?

4

Work in a group of three.

a Prepare a list of questions that you think the interviewer asked the young people.
b Take the role of one of the young people each. Find out from the article what you can about this person, e.g. ambitions, relations with parents etc.
c Interview each other.

5

Work in a group. Imagine that five years have passed. Write a short article with the title *Five years on . . .* . In your article say what happened to the three young people.

In their words...

PAUL ADAMS, 16, reckons his life will change dramatically during the next five years.

"I want to get some A Levels if my GCSE exam results are good enough. I have left all my options open and have no idea what I'm going to do when I leave school. Getting a job and keeping it is very important in this area."

Student governor **CARL MERRITT**, 17, has just re-sat his GCSE exams because he didn't get high enough grades to train as a trading standards officer.

"I really want to do this job so I need to get the right qualifications," he says.

He gets on very well with his mum and dad. "They always let me make decisions about my future and I respect their views."

KAREN WILLIAMS, 16, wants to become a teacher. She says her parents have been a great influence on her choice of career.

"I have to wait for the results of my GCSEs before I can finally decide what I do. Ideally, I'd like to take A Levels.

Section C

1

Read the article quickly.

a Who do you think it is written for?

b Who do you think it is written by?

the CONFIDENCE factor

Whether you're seeking your first job, looking for a new career move or trying to get back into work after a spell away from employment, you need to be well-prepared.

Personal confidence, the ability to present yourself to others, and a knowledge of the local job market are all part of successful job hunting. Read on for more...

Tips for Practical Job Hunting

The skill in job hunting lies in persuading an employer that you've got the knowledge, skills and attitudes to be a useful member of his or her workforce.

You've got to believe in yourself before an employer will believe in you. So think positively! Try writing a list of statements starting 'I think I would make a good employee because...' It may sound like a weird thing to do, but it can be very confidence-boosting.

Remember... accentuate the postive.

Get together with a friend, and help one another draft application letters and CVs. Read through your school or youth training record of achievement, and remind yourself of all the good qualities you have to offer an employer.

> I would make a good worker because I keep cool in a crisis.

> I would make a good employee because I'm always cheerful.

> I would make a good employee because I like meeting people.

> I would make a good employee because I enjoy sorting out mechanical problems like when Mick's car broke down.

2

List three things which are important in 'the confidence factor'. Which of these factors do you think is the most important?

3

Which of these jobs would suit the four speakers in the text best?

a police officer   d nurse

b car mechanic   e accountant

c shop assistant   f social worker

4

Work with a partner.

a Choose a job for your partner and complete this sentence about him or her: 'I think (partner's name) would make a good (type of job) because . . .'

b Now choose a job for yourself and complete this sentence:
'I think I would make a good (type of job) because . . .'

c Now compare what you and your partner have written about each other.

5

Read about Jean Attree and put these events in the right order.

- does A-level course
- completes course at North London Polytechnic
- leaves school
- becomes self-employed photographer
- works in office

6

How did these people/ organisations help Jean?

a her friends
b her local Jobcentre
c South Thames TEC
d other photographers

7

What did Jean feel were the advantages and disadvantages of becoming self-employed?

8

Which of these things a) has Jean learnt to do, b) does Jean hope to do?
Write them under the correct heading, a) or b).

- run a business
- deal with customers
- get commissions for magazines
- photograph record covers
- build up the business
- work with other photographers

9

Work with a partner.

a Think of one more question you would like to ask Jean.
b Decide how she would answer it.

10

Choose a title for this article.

Jean Attree recently set up as a professional photographer, turning a hobby into her business.

I've always enjoyed photography and it is something where you learn a lot from experience. Friends told me that my pictures were good, and encouraged me to try and make a living at it. I started in October, and I'm building up confidence and contacts. I've also had work assisting other photographers which is a good way to learn.

I've done various commissions, but at the moment I'm developing my portfolio so that I can get work doing album covers and commissions for magazines. I like doing portraits and I enjoy black and white photography, but colour work pays better.'

As she was unemployed, her local Jobcentre put her in touch with the enterprise team at South Thames TEC (Training and Enterprise Council). They were able to give her an enterprise allowance of £40 per week to help her get started.

'I was one of those people who couldn't wait to leave school. At 16 I went into a boring office job which I hated. I started to think that doing a degree would widen my options. I did a one year part-time A level course, and then at 24 went to North London Polytechnic to do a degree in French and film studies. Having had experience of working, I was keen to make the most of the opportunity to study.

As the course came to an end I still wasn't sure what I wanted to do. Self employment appealed to me as it offered challenge and variety, though I knew there wouldn't be paid holidays or sick leave. Since I started I've learned a lot about the practical aspects of running a business and marketing myself. I'm getting better at dealing with customers – in knowing what they are looking for. I'm hoping the business will build up steadily.'

Section D

1

Work with a partner. Look at the photograph.
Discuss with your partner the question: *What is
he?* Now read the poem.

What Is He?

What is he?
– A man, of course.
Yes, but what does he do?
– He lives and is a man.
Oh quite! but he must work. He must have a job of some sort.
– Why?
Because obviously he's not one of the leisured classes.
– I don't know. He has lots of leisure. And he makes quite
   beautiful chairs.
There you are then! He's a cabinet maker.
– No no!
Anyhow a carpenter and joiner.
– Not at all.
But you said so.
– What did I say?
That he made chairs, and was a joiner and carpenter.
– I said he made chairs, but I did not say he was a carpenter.
All right then, he's just an amateur.
– Perhaps! Would you say a thrush was a professional flautist,
   or just an amateur?
I'd say it was just a bird.
– And I say he is just a man.
All right! You always did quibble.

D. H. Lawrence

2

What does the man in the poem do for a living?

3

The first speaker's argument seems to be that
someone's identity is defined by his job. What is
the second speaker's argument? Who do you
agree with?

4

a Do you think the word *quibble* means to . . . ?

   1 agree with the other person
   2 argue over small things

b How do the two speakers resolve their
   different opinions?

Project

*Work in groups to produce a short report on work
in your country.*
a *Research facts and figures and produce a
   factfile.*
b *Devise your own questionnaire to ask other
   people in your class (or other classes) about
   their attitudes to work. Draw a chart (or charts)
   and write a summary of your findings.*

Facts, opinions, and advertisements

Why are the British such keen readers of newspapers? Does it matter that Britain is turning into a nation of television addicts? And why do people all over the world tune in to the BBC World Service?

Section A

The British are voracious newspaper readers, reading more newspapers than any other European country, and some of our 'quality' papers are among the best in the world. However, the gap between 'quality' papers like *The Times* and 'tabloids' like *The Sun* is wide and getting wider. This gap reflects the immense social and educational differences that still persist in British society. While quality papers like *The Independent* and *The Guardian* give their readers an in-depth background to crucial issues of the day, tabloids like *The Sun* and *The Mirror* provide a steady diet of gossip and trivia. In-between papers like the *Daily Mail* cover a good deal of news in a popular way.

The quality papers sell from 300,000 to 1 million copies each a day, the middle-of-the-road papers sell around 2 million copies each a day, while the tabloids have circulations of up to 4 million copies a day. Why is there this division between the quality and the popular press? What does it tell us about the British press? What does it tell us about Britain today?

1
Read the article.
Match the names of the newspapers in the photographs with the descriptions below.

a quality
b tabloid
c middle-of-the-road

2
Work with a partner. Discuss possible answers to the three questions asked in the last paragraph of the article.

3
Read the article again quickly

a Find the names of six British newspapers.
b Divide them into quality papers and tabloids.

4
Find expressions in the article that mean the following:

a very keen
b shows
c very important
d unimportant news

5
In pairs write three sentences summarising the most important points made in the article.

6
a Write a headline for the article.
b Work in a group. Compare your headlines. Choose the best ones.

Section B

1

Read these two articles about television viewing habits in Britain. Which article tells you about . . . ?

a people's leisure activities
b the decline in television viewing
c the effects of television on family life

IT IS possible that television is losing its magic, and we are witnessing the beginnings of a return to print, or even the radio, according to a report on social habits published today. "After 30 years of spectacular growth television may be on the wane," the report from the Henley Centre for Forecasting says.

The report points to the decline of 5 per cent in total average viewing in the 5 years to 1989. By 1989 the average had dropped to just under 25 hours a week, a net weekly loss of one hour 14 minutes.

"By any objective criterion, the average 3.5 hours a day we spend in front of the set (the highest in Europe) must be the mark of a couch potato society gone mad."

THE couch-potato cat and the square-eyed dog emerge as the innocent victims in a survey this week of the nation's leisure habits.

Most people watch television for most of their leisure time, although other pursuits – eating, reading, sleeping and arguing – are frequently conducted at the same time.

The survey by National Opinion Polls for the Radio Times found that for more than 5 million people, television is virtually their only leisure pursuit: for 12 per cent of those asked, it occupied more than 90 per cent of their leisure time. More than 8 million pets watch.

Despite, or because of, the amount of peoples' lives it devours, the stigma attached to television watching persists. While half the population admit to using it to relax, and the same percentage could not live happily without one (and 66 per cent without radio), three-quarters think that other people rely on it too much.

Only 12 per cent read for 10 hours a week or more, and 83 per cent read for less than three hours a week; 14 per cent spend 7 hours a week or more on exercise, 28 per cent less than 7 hours, and 43 per cent no time at all.

A third say they do absolutely nothing for up to 3 hours a week, and 12 per cent say they spend 10 hours a week doing nothing much.

By comparison a third watch for over 3 hours a day, a fifth over 5 hours, and 7 per cent for 11 hours a day or more. Women and the elderly watch most.

The survey does suggest, however, that television does not destroy family life. Nearly three-quarters of those asked, particularly those with children or who are in social categories A and B, watch mostly with family or friends, and programmes are a topic of conversation.

2

Complete these sentences with information from the articles. Does any of the information surprise you?

a .... million people spend most of their leisure time watching TV.
b 8 million .... watch TV.
c .... per cent of the people interviewed in the survey do nothing for up to three hours a week.
d The popularity of TV is ....
e The average person watches TV for .... hours a week.
f People in .... watch more TV than in any other European country.

Project

Work in a group to carry out a survey on TV watching habits.

a *Devise a questionnaire.*
b *Interview people from another class.*
c *Analyse the results of the questionnaire.*
d *Write a report summarising your findings.*

Section C

1

Look at the women in these
advertisements.

a What do you think each of
   them is advertising?

b Which adjectives would you
   choose to describe each
   woman?

  1 attractive
  2 powerful
  3 provocative
  4 nice
  5 interesting
  6 old-fashioned
  7 smart
  8 cheerful

c Work with a partner and
   discuss your choices.

2

Work in a group. How do you
think women are generally
presented in advertising?

a fairly
b mainly as sex objects
c only in a few stereotyped
   roles (e.g. housewife,
   girlfriend)

3

Work with a partner. Read this
report of a complaint to the
Advertising Standards
Authority. Do you agree with
the ASA's decision?

4

Work in a group. Discuss these
questions.

a How are women shown in
   advertisements in your
   country?

b Is this advertising sexist?

c Which particular
   advertisements do you
   like/dislike?

Complaint:
**There were objections to an advertisement in poster form
for half-price night time electricity featuring a naked
woman showering in a telephone box. The complainants
objected that the use of the naked woman was gratuitous
and offensive.**

Conclusion: Complaints upheld.
The advertisers stated that the illustration of the woman taking a
shower was to demonstrate the benefits of cheap hot water and in
their view contained no sexual or sensuous implications. The
Authority considered that the use of nudity in connection with
showers was not in itself objectionable and accepted that the
illustration in question was not particularly sexual. It considered,
however, that the image of a woman naked in a telephone box was
inappropriate in the context since the advertisement was for electric
hot water rather than for a shower and furthermore did not invite
telephone enquiries. It requested the advertisers to reconsider the
presentation of future advertisements.

Section D

1

The five sentences below have been deleted from the factfile. Read the factfile and decide where the sentences go.

a The BBC has five national radio channels.
b In 1991 the annual fee was £71.
c It has an estimated audience of 120 million listeners.
d There are no commercials on BBC television.
e In 1991 this stood at £122 million a year.

2

Work with a partner. What similarities and differences are there between broadcasting in Britain and broadcasting in your country?

3

Read this information about the BBC World Service. Does it answer these questions?

a How many hours a day does the World Service broadcast?
b What types of programmes does it broadcast?

The World Service of the British Broadcasting Corporation broadcasts in 37 languages from the heart of London, reaching a wider global audience than any other radio station. The World Service's regular audience figure totals 120 million a week.

Of these listeners, 25 million listen to the 24-hour World Service in English and 100 million to broadcasts in other languages, while 5 million listen to both.

These are listeners who appreciate the accuracy and impartiality of the BBC's comprehensive news and current affairs coverage. They also enjoy the range of features, sport, business, science and technology, music, drama, religion and light entertainment which the station has to offer.

BBC World Service 1990

4

Write sentences about the BBC World Service using the figures below.

a 5 million
b 25 million
c 120 million

5

Work in a group. What do you think is the most important feature of the BBC World Service?

Factfile | Radio and TV

1
The British Broadcasting Corporation (BBC) has two television channels – BBC 1 and BBC 2; the Independent Broadcasting Authority (IBA) has one channel – ITV. In addition, there is another independent commercial channel – Channel 4.

2
The BBC gets its funds from a licence fee which all owners of televisions must pay. In 1990 there were 19.5 million TV licences.

3
The IBA channels are funded by television advertisements (commercials).

4
Commercials occur at breaks within and between programmes.

5
Political and religious commercials are forbidden, as are advertisements for tobacco.

6
Although neither the BBC nor the IBA is Government-controlled, they *are* subject to Government directives. Thus, for example, since 1988 the Government has banned television interviews with members of the IRA.

7
Both the BBC and the IBA produce educational programmes for schools.

8
Sixty-eight per cent of British households rent or own a video-cassette recorder.

9
Radio 1 broadcasts pop music, Radio 2 has easy listening music, Radio 3 specialises in classical music and cricket, Radio 4 in news, drama, and current affairs, Radio 5 is devoted to sport and education. It also broadcasts several hours of BBC World Service.

10
There are a number of independent and local radio stations. Many of these are intended to reach specialised audiences.

11
The BBC World Service is funded by a grant from the Foreign and Commonwealth Office.

12
The World Service broadcasts in 37 languages for a combined total of 785 hours a week.

The classical boom

Who cares about classical music? Well, the thousands of people who flock to the 'Proms' every year do. So do the millions who buy Nigel Kennedy's records of Brahms and Vivaldi. What effect has Nigel had on youngsters in Britain today?

Section A

1

Work in groups. Look at the CD covers. Do you know who is featured on each CD?

a Do you know anything about these people?
b What type of music is popular in your country? What sort of music do you listen to?

Section B

1

Work with a partner. Look at the page from the Prom programme. What do you think the Proms are?

a Which of the five things in the programme would you find most annoying if you were at the Proms?

b Act out a conversation in which one of you complains to the other about his/her annoying behaviour during a Prom performance.

c Write one more request to include in the programme.

Please do not drink ...

... or eat during the performance, as this is distracting both to the performers and to other members of the audience

Please ensure that all alarms are switched off before the concert begins

FIVE THINGS WE ASK YOU NOT TO DO AT THE PROMS

The taking of photographs in the hall is strictly forbidden

This Prom is being broadcast live on BBC Radio 3, and the first half live on the World Service. We therefore ask members of the audience to act as if in a recording studio for the duration of the concert, and to maintain ABSOLUTE SILENCE during the performance of the music

Latecomers will not be admitted unless or until there is a suitable break in the music. There is a stereo relay in the foyer of Door 6 for those who arrive after the concert has begun

Please try not to cough during the music

2

Read the article on the right. How did the Proms get their name?

3

Read the article again. What did these people do?

a Sir Henry Wood
b Andrew Davis
c Sir Edward Elgar

4

a Do you know which song this verse comes from?

> *Land of Hope and Glory,*
> *Mother of the Free,*
> *How shall we extol thee,*
> *who are born of thee?*
> *Wider still and wider shall*
> *thy bounds be set;*
> *God who made thee mighty,*
> *make thee mightier yet.*

b 1 Who does *thee* refer to?
   2 What does the third line mean?

    a our country should become more powerful
    b our country should invade other countries
    c our country's values should spread all over the world

c How would you describe the words of this song?

    1 nationalistic
    2 patriotic
    3 racist
    4 sacreligious
    5 imperialist

5

Look at the cartoon. What might the man be saying?

In 1894 Sir Henry Wood conducted the first Promenade Concert in London. His aim was to make classical music more popular and to encourage young people to get to know the great masters of the classical repertory – Mozart, Bach, Beethoven. In order to make the atmosphere more informal, people were allowed to stand and even walk around – 'promenade' – during the concert. Seats were cheap and the crowds flocked to attend.

Now, the Proms, as they are usually called, make up the most important annual classical music festival in Britain. In 1990 between 20 July and 15 September there were sixty-six Proms, with music ranging from Trinidadian steel bands to concert performances of operas by Gluck, Mozart, and Janáček. The 3,000 seat Albert Hall was 85% full throughout the season. Tickets for the 'Last Night' were sold out before the Proms started.

The Last Night of the Proms is a special occasion. It has become a British institution. The atmosphere is electric. The Albert Hall is filled to capacity with thousands of people, most of them young, many carrying flags, banners, and balloons, all of them eager to have a good time. One of the pieces traditionally played at the Last Night is a march written by Sir Edward Elgar in 1902 called 'Pomp and Circumstance'. A.C. Benson wrote words to Elgar's march and under its new title 'Land of Hope and Glory', it became an immensely popular patriotic hymn – a kind of alternative National Anthem. Now it has been taken up by the Promenaders, as the young concert-goers are known. On the Last Night, they join in the chorus, singing lustily and waving Union Jacks – a bit like football supporters!

The Last Night of the Proms can be a nerve-racking experience for the conductor of the orchestra. Andrew Davis conducted his first Last Night in 1988:

> *I had been full of apprehension right up till the last minute: it's such an institution, and there are so many more facets to it than just conducting the music. Then they opened the door, and there was this sea of humanity in front of me with everyone in festive mood: so I thought, well, I'm just going to go out there and enjoy it.*

Proms ride a wave of classical popularity

WHAT YOU longed for is yours, sang the Madonna-figure, as an audience of thousands – standing room only – strained to catch a glimpse. And this was only the warm-up. Fifteen minutes later the show turned into a celebration of the body and the new life, with a huge choir roaring in ecstasy and gongs crashing. Mahler's Resurrection Symphony had climaxed, and the first night of the 1989 Proms was reaching its triumphant end.

This year's season begins as attempts to give classical music mass appeal are reaching new highs. Earlier this month Luciano Pavarotti was shooting up the popular music charts and the London Chamber Orchestra packed the Hammersmith Odeon with a concert of Vivaldi and Tchaikovsky which were played "seriously loud".

This is the 96th opening for the Proms, one of the longest-lasting successes in popularising music. Many concerts are already sold out except for the "promenade" or standing tickets and queues for those often start hours before. How far the social spread has broadened over the years is not clear. Certainly the 'hooligan' factor on the Last Night remains determinedly up-market as the massed middle classes shout their rival tribal cries of "Heave!" and "Ho!" and sing their equivalents of "Ere we go" ("Land of Hope and Glory") and "You'll never walk alone" ("Jerusalem").

Last year the BBC, which runs the Proms, did its first market research on audiences. They are younger than other concert audiences, with a larger proportion aged under 25 and a smaller one over 44. They are also more male: the same balance of the sexes as the population as a whole, rather than being weighted towards women. One in five had been to a pop concert in the previous year, and one in two to opera. Most come because of the programme or "because it's a Prom"; 5 per cent for the orchestra, and 4 per cent for the conductor – a relative score which will go down well with players.

Meanwhile the Proms reach their biggest public on radio and television: 65 out of 66 go out live on Radio 3, 20 on the World Service, four on BBC1 or BBC2, and six as televised recorded highlights.

6

a Read the headline of the article. Do you think classical music is becoming more or less popular in Britain?

b Read the article and see if you were right.

7

Read the article again. What kind of people go to the Proms? Why do they go to the Proms?

8

a Write captions for the three photographs.

b Work in a group. Compare your captions. Choose the best ones.

9

Work with a partner. Would you like to go to the Proms? Why?/Why not?

Section C

1

Read these two newspaper articles.

a Which article appeared in May?

b Which article appeared in August?

c Which article is an advertisement?

d What is the connection between the two articles?

2

Work with a partner. Read one article each and find out what makes Nigel different from other violinists. Tell your partner.

3

a Work with your partner again. Read your article once more and find out what it tells you about the concert.

1 date   4 price of tickets
2 time   5 concertos
3 venue   6 audience capacity

b Compare your notes with those of your partner. Which article tells you more? Why is this?

4

What was the weather like on August 19th? What do these expressions mean?

a shower   d bucketed
b raindrops   down
c thunder   e damp

5

Imagine you went to the concert on August 19th. Write a letter to a friend describing what the concert was like.

Sample Nigel's string fever

A young man in pointy boots, leather jacket and jeans is changing the traditional image of classical music.

He is an extraordinary phenomenon; a colourful youth who has engineered a cult following without for a moment cheapening the beauty of what he plays.

Now he is preparing to play the concert of a lifetime. It will take place on Sunday, August 19 at the Crystal Palace Bowl in south-east London, an open-air auditorium with a grass slope leading to the stage.

There will be up to 25,000 in the audience who will hear him play both a Bruch concerto and *The Four Seasons*, accompanied by the English Chamber Orchestra.

This unique event, which is one of the musical highlights of the year, has been arranged in association with The Daily Mail.

The concert starts at 6.30pm (gates open 4.30pm) and will last for about three and a half hours. Tickets cost £16 each or you can buy special £55 Gold Tickets which include a buffet and champagne in the VIP marquee.

HOW TO GET YOUR TICKETS

BOOK your tickets now by ringing
071-818 6131
(manned 24-hour service).
No booking fee payable.
(Please allow six weeks for delivery of tickets)

VIVALDI KEEPS SPIRITS UP AS RAINDROPS BUCKET DOWN

Kennedy lifts a damp audience

By SPENCER BRIGHT

AS Nigel Kennedy took up his bow, a five-minute shower began to fall.

He did ask for it, playing a few bars of *Raindrops Keep Falling on My Head* when he appeared on stage at the Crystal Palace Bowl with the English Chamber Orchestra.

It had been the wettest day for over two months. The weather held for most of the show through to the encore. Then it bucketed down. What was remarkable in this most unrock concert-like audience was their stoicism. They were determined to enjoy themselves, cuddling under plastic sheeting and tentatively opening their picnic ice boxes. It was an eccentric English garden party.

Vivaldi's *The Four Seasons* was the biggest draw in the show. I found it rather subdued. The summer movement, with an intense passage ideally conveying the oppression of summer heat, sounded somewhat damp.

But there is no doubting Kennedy is a real star. His personality is a magnet for all generations. And there was more of a family closeness at this concert than you would find at any other classical performance. Kennedy has more than achieved his aim of popularising the classics.

Singing in the rain with girlfriend Brix
Picture: JENNY GOODALL

'Miles better?'

Glasgow was once known only as the capital of crime and deprivation, but now it's bustling with art galleries, concert halls, bars and boutiques. The old Glasgow, for all its poverty, had a warm heart. Is it still beating?

Section A

1

Work with a partner.

a Read the factfile and select the three most interesting facts about Glasgow.

b Work in a group. Discuss the facts you have listed. Have you selected the same facts or different ones? Try to agree on a final choice of facts and compare these with other groups' choices.

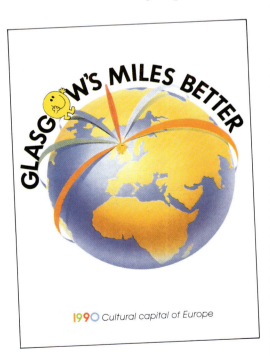

GLASGOW'S MILES BETTER

1990 Cultural capital of Europe

*F*actfile | Glasgow

1
Glasgow has a cathedral that was founded in 1125 and a university that was founded in 1451.

2
In the 19th century Glasgow became one the most important industrial cities in the world, particularly as a centre for shipbuilding.

3
Glasgow is situated on the River Clyde. The Clyde was widened to enable bigger and bigger ships to be built. People used to say: *Glasgow made the Clyde and the Clyde made Glasgow.*

4
Until the middle of this century it was the second-biggest city in the British Empire with a population of over 1 million people. Now the population of Glasgow is 700,000.

5
Although Glasgow is the largest city in Scotland, Edinburgh, with a population of around 400,000, is the capital. The two cities are friendly rivals.

6
In the 19th and early 20th century Glasgow was a dirty old town full of decaying buildings and run-down factories. Today many of the old warehouses and small factories have been converted into smart shops.

7
More than £40 million was invested in the arts in Glasgow for its year as European City of Culture in 1990. The main expenditure was on a new £26 million concert hall in the centre of the city.

8
Twenty miles north of Glasgow is Loch Lomond, the largest lake in Britain.

9
Glasgow has the biggest football stadium in Britain, Hampden Park. It can seat well over 100,000.

10
In 1983 Queen Elizabeth II opened the Burrell Collection, a fabulous array of art treasures from all around the world which has become a big tourist attraction in Scotland.

Section B

1

Read this short article about the Burrell Collection and find out what makes it unique.

2

a Which three objects from the Burrell Collection do these captions refer to?

   1 statue of Egyptian goddess

   2 stained glass of archangel blowing trumpet

   3 Indian carpet

b One object is uncaptioned. Write a caption for it.

This 15th century Chinese statue of a disciple of Buddha is one of the glories of the Burrell Collection. The Burrell Collection consists of hundreds of paintings, tapestries, sculptures, stained glass, carpets and other valuable objects from all over the world and from every period of history. What makes the Burrell Collection unique is that it reflects the taste of one man, Sir William Burrell (1861–1958), who put the collection together over a period of some fifty years.

In 1967 a large estate in the countryside just outside Glasgow, was donated to the city and it was decided to house the collection there. Work began on the building in 1978 and the gallery was opened in 1983. Less than a year later the Burrell Collection received its millionth visitor and it is now the leading tourist attraction in the whole of Scotland.

Project

Produce a brochure to attract tourists to visit a city in your country. Your brochure should focus on areas such as these:

a the attractions of the city, e.g. famous buildings, museums, parks

b events taking place in the city this year

c historical associations of the city, e.g. famous events, writers, artists

d nearby places of interest, e.g. villages, mountains, lakes

Think of a slogan for your campaign to attract tourists. Design a logo for the city.

Section C

1

Work with a partner. Look at the photograph of the Glasgow children and discuss these questions.

a Do you think these children are friends or members of the same family?

b Was this photograph taken

 1 in the last five years?
 2 about fifty years ago?
 3 a hundred years ago?

c Which word best describes the children?
 happy   poor   tragic
 dirty   healthy

2

Now read this short text and check your answers.

This photograph of the Samson children, taken in 1962, brings together two great Glasgow artists, neither of them born in Scotland. Oscar Marzaroli took the photo of the children in the studio of Joan Eardley, the painter.

3

Read these notes about the two artists. Find as many similarities as you can between their lives.

Oscar Marzaroli
1933: born Castiglione Vara, Italy
1935: family moves to Glasgow
    Oscar studies at Glasgow School of Art
    works as photo-journalist in Stockholm and London
1959: returns to Glasgow
    founds photographic studio – 'Studio 59'
1967–1983: film producer/director, makes 70+ films
1988: *Shades of Grey*, collection of his photographs 1956–1987, published
    dies 26 August

Joan Eardley
1921: born Guildford, Surrey
1929: father dies (suicide)
1940: family moves to Glasgow, Joan studies at Glasgow School of Art
1947: first exhibition of paintings
1952: moves into studio in Townhead district of Glasgow
    starts painting Glasgow street life and kids
    becomes friends with the Samson family
1961: becomes ill with cancer, continues painting
1963: elected to Royal Scottish Academy
    dies 16 August

4

Use the notes to write brief biographies of the two artists.

5

Compare Marzaroli's photograph of the children with Eardley's painting of them.

6

Read the poem by Glasgow poet, Edwin Morgan, reflecting on what it means to him to own one of Joan Eardley's paintings now the scenes she pictured have vanished.

7

Match these parts of the poem with their descriptions (a–d) below.

part 1 (lines 1–12)   part 3 (lines 23–30)
part 2 (lines 13–22)   part 4 (lines 31–32)

a The children live on in the painting.
b The painting is described.
c Paintings have the ability to preserve things that no longer exist.
d The houses in the painting have now been demolished and no-one lives there now.

To Joan Eardley

1   Pale yellow letters
    humbly straggling across
    the once brilliant red
    of a broken shop-face
    CONFECTIO
    and a blur of children
    at their games, passing,
    gazing as they pass
    at the blur of sweets
10 in the dingy, cosy
    Rottenrow[1] window –
    an Eardley on my wall.
    Such rags and streaks
    that master us! –
    that fix what the pick
    and bulldozer have crumbled
    to a dingier dust,
    the living blur
    fiercely guarding
20 energy that has vanished,
    cries filling still
    the unechoing close!
    I wandered by the rubble
    and the houses left standing
    kept a chill, dying life
    in their islands of stone.
    No window opened
    as the coal cart rolled
    and the coalman's call
30 fell coldly to the ground.
    But the shrill children
    jump on my wall.

1 *Rottenrow* = a poor district of Glasgow

8

dingy = dark and gloomy, *cosy* = comfortable. How can *dingy* and *cosy* (line 10) be used to describe the same thing?

9

a Find words in Section 3 (lines 23–30) which suggest death/destruction.
b Find words in the same section which suggest life and survival.

10

How have towns and cities in your country changed in recent years?

Streets of London

With the highest percentage of home ownership in Europe, why are there increasing numbers of homeless on the streets in Britain?

Section A

SOUTH CAMBRIDGESHIRE	GLEN AFFRIC, SCOTLAND	DEPTFORD	WEST WIMBLEDON	FOREST HILL SE23
3 bedroomed detached bungalow, quiet village cul-de-sac, large plot, double garage, conservatory, GCH, stone fireplace, luxury fitted kitchen, fitted bedroom, 5 miles Cambridge. Convenient shops, amenities. **£87,500**	Traditional stone-built cottage in conservation village in the most beautiful glen in Scotland. 1/4 acre garden, 2 receptions, 3 bedrooms, kitchen, bathroom, Full Central Heating. Inverness 25 miles. **£46,000 ONO**	Two bedroomed Grade II listed first floor flat. Georgian circa 1780, 30 seconds river, Central Heating. Close to tubes, buses, shopping. Garden, off-road parking. Not Docklands. **£59,950 ONO**	1920's 3 bedroomed house in quiet cul-de-sac. Well maintained throughout. 17 foot fully fitted kitchen, 2 receptions, UPVC double glazing replacement windows. Small sunny 30 foot garden. **£102,950**	Spacious Edwardian 4 bedroomed semi-detached. Many original features, quiet road. Beautiful 29ft lounge, second reception, excellent decorative order. Sunny garden. Close BR (15 mins London Bridge). **£142,500**

1

Look at the advertisements above for properties in Britain and find the following:

a a house in Scotland
b an 18th-century flat
c a four-bedroomed house
d a house with a big garden
e a house with double glazing
f a house with a conservatory
g the cheapest house
h the most expensive house

First-time buyer Jan Healey bought her two-bedroomed flat in a Victorian terraced house in south-west London at the height of the property boom in 1988. She paid £83,000 and spent a further £15,000 on refurbishment. It has been on the market for 20 months, much admired; but two offers have fallen through and the original asking price of £89,950 has now dropped to £79,950.

VICTORIAN CHARM – ANY OFFERS?

"I LIKE the area," says Jan Healey. "You can see the common from here; there are masses of restaurants and it's only 10 minutes' walk to the railway station. The flat's layout is unusual – you go down from the sitting-room into the kitchen. It had lots of potential."

The flat, a middle-floor conversion in Battersea, was given a complete face-lift when Ms Healey bought it in 1988. Out went the brown and cream décor. In came fresh blues, yellows and pinks. The second bedroom became a dining-room. Carpets, tiling and appliances were replaced. Jan Healey installed shelving, cupboards, new lighting, a shower system; she repapered walls, hand-dragged kitchen units, had curtains and sofas tailor-made. The final bill was £15,000. Yet this pretty little flat will

2

Look at the photograph and read the caption.

a How much money did the woman spend on improving her flat?

b How long has she been trying to sell it?

c How much has the value of the flat changed in that time?

3

Read the article and answer these questions.

a What are the advantages of Jan Healey's flat?

b What do you think is the most important change Jan has made to the flat?

c Why do you think Jan can't sell her flat?

   1 it's too expensive
   2 it's a buyer's market
   3 buyers don't know what they want
   4 people don't like the way the flat is laid out

d Why doesn't Jan stop trying to sell her flat?

4

Which of these opinions do you agree with most?

a 'I feel really sorry for Jan Healey, she tried to make her flat really nice and now she's going to lose a lot of money on it. And it's not her fault.'

b 'I feel a bit sorry for her, but I think she could try harder to sell her flat. She could lower the price a bit more or advertise it better. Put a big sign up outside, for instance.'

c 'I don't feel sorry for her at all. At least she's got somewhere to live and it's worth a lot of money. What about all the people who don't have any homes and have to sleep on the streets? That's who I feel sorry for!'

5

Read the factfile and complete it with the figures given below:

- 150,000   195,000
- 7%   66%   72%
- £62,000

not sell. It has sat on estate agents' books for over a year and a half. The asking price today is just £79,950. "The two-bedroomed flat market in this area of London rose the highest in the boom and has dropped the lowest, in some cases up to 28 per cent of 1988 values," says Olivia Fennell of agents Barnard Marcus.

Jan Healey's flat went up for sale in February 1990 for £89,950. Already the market was slipping and recouping her costs was out of the question. "The initial response was good," she says. "I was getting five or six people a week looking round." A couple quickly offered £86,000 and they got as far as the drafting of contracts, so Ms Healey made an offer on another flat. Everything collapsed when her prospective buyers failed to get a mortgage.

She instructed another agent and lowered the price to its present £79,950. People come to view at the rate of one or two a week, but still nobody buys. "I wonder whether I should take it off the market," says Jan Healey, "but I still believe someone will come along and fall madly in love with it."

F*actfile* | **Housing**

In 1990, ... houses were built by the private sector (commercial builders), and approximately a quarter of this figure, (47,000), by the public sector (local government housing authorities).

Shelter, a charity which looks after the homeless, estimates that more than .... people under the age of 25 are homeless for at least a short period in any given year.

Between 1971 and 1991, the proportion of people who owned their own homes rose from 50% to ...., a rise of 16%. This is the highest percentage in Europe.

There are now more than 15 million owner-occupied homes in Great Britain.

Owner-occupiers are entitled to tax relief on mortgages of up to £30,000.

The average value of a three-bedroomed house in Britain in 1992 was ...., but in large areas of the south-east such properties are worth at least twice that price.

If an owner-occupier fails to keep up his/her mortgage repayments, the building society may take possession of his/her house. In 1991, 75,400 houses were repossessed by building societies. This was a massive increase of .... over 1990.

The proportion of privately-rented accommodation declined from over 50% in 1951 to just over .... in 1991.

Section B

1

Look at the photograph.

a Where is the man?
b What is he doing?

2

a Which of these statements do you agree with?

1 'Poor man. He's got nowhere to live.'
2 'Why doesn't he get a job?'
3 'Some of these beggars earn £100 a day, you know.'
4 'Thank goodness I'm not homeless. I'm lucky to have a roof over my head.'
5 'It's disgraceful that everyone doesn't have a home of their own. The Government should do something about it.'
6 'Why doesn't he go back and live with his family?'

b Work in a group. Discuss your opinions.

3

Work in your group again. Are there people like the man in the photograph in your country? Why are they homeless? Are they given any help? What kind of help?

Section C

1

Work with a partner.

a How significant are these factors in causing homelessness?

1 lack of money
2 parent-children quarrels
3 divorce

b Can you think of any other causes of homelessness?

2

Look at the diagram 'Why homeless?' How important are the factors you discussed in contributing to homelessness among the four groups of people described?

3

Answer these questions.

a What is the most common cause of homelessness?

b Which two reasons for homelessness are directly linked to *homes*?

c What is the difference between a home with a *landlord* and *tenant* and a home with an *owner-occupier*?

d Which group of homeless people is increasing the fastest?

Why homeless?

Some of the reasons why people become homeless

People become homeless because they cannot find accommodation which is suitable for them, and which they can afford. There are many reasons which explain how people become homeless:

Families/friends falling out: 43%

Many young people in particular become homeless because they are no longer able or willing to live with their parents. Some people have to leave their homes because they find they are unable to share accommodation with friends.

Partners separating: 17%

The second most common cause of homelessness is the break down of marriages or relationships. When a couple splits up, one or both partners are often left with no home.

Landlord problems: 12%

About one in eight people who become homeless do so because they are forced to leave their privately rented homes. Landlords have the power to evict tenants after their agreed tenancy period has finished.

Cannot pay mortgage: 6%

The fastest-growing group of homeless people comprises those who have lost homes which they owned themselves. Owner-occupiers are vulnerable because of high interest rates, which have pushed up their mortgage repayments. In 1989, more than 47,000 families lost their homes because they fell behind with their mortgages.

Brian (16). His parents threw him out.

'We'd had disagreements. I didn't want to conform and that was that. I wasn't a great guy at home. I don't blame my family.'

Malcom (40), a bricklayer.

'I had a terrible year. My mother died and then my son got killed in a hit-and-run accident. I got into debt and my business started to go down-hill. My wife left me and I started drinking and that made everything worse.'

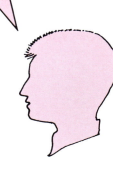

Cathy (16), ran away from a children's home.

'I can't go back to the home and I don't want to go back to my foster-parents. I know I could go into one of the night shelters, but I don't like the rules – you've got to be in by eight o'clock at night.'

4
Read the quotations from three homeless people. Which category of homelessness do they fit into?

5
Work in a group of four. Look back at the causes of homelessness shown in the diagram. Choose one cause each. Take turns to give advice to each other.
Is the advice you are given by the others in your group good advice?

Project

Work in a group to design a poster which draws attention to the plight of the homeless.
a *Choose a charity (real or imaginary) that needs/wants to raise money.*
b *Decide on the 'message' of your poster. Write the text and find photographs or draw pictures for the poster. (Use facts from this unit if you like.)*
c *Display your poster on the classroom walls.*

Love and marriage?

Years ago people often married young, had children quickly, and got to know each other as they went along. Now many people marry later, sometimes after living together first. Surely this should make marriages more stable? And yet the British divorce rate continues to rise.

Section A

1

Work with a partner. Ask and answer these questions together.

a Where do you live?
b Who else lives in your house or flat?

You're going to read the words of a song called *Our house* by the pop group 'Madness'. Write down five words you expect to find in it.

2

Read the first verse of the song.

a How many people do you think live in the house?
b Who's tired?
c Who's impatient?

3

Read the second verse.

a Which of these words describe *our house*?
   busy   clean   dull   friendly   noisy
b What do you think *house-proud* means?

4

a The lines of the last verse of the song have been mixed up. Put them in the right order.
b Now check your answer on page 90.

5

Which of the houses in these photographs comes closest to your idea of the house in the song?

Our house

Father wears his Sunday best,
Mother's tired, she needs a rest.
The kids are playing up¹ downstairs,
Sister's sighing in her sleep.
Brother's got a date to keep,
He can't hang around².

Our house it has a crowd,
There's always something happening,
And it's usually quite loud.
Our Mum, she's so house-proud,
Nothing ever slows her down
And a mess is not allowed.

Then she sends the kids to school
Mother has to iron his shirt
In lots of ways.
She's the one they're going to miss
Father gets up late for work
Sees them off with a small kiss.

¹ *playing up* = misbehaving
² *hang around* = wait

Section B

1

Read this short article about marriage today.

a Who is Martin Whyte?
b Why is he mentioned?

> **W**HENEVER modern thinkers turn their attention to the condition of marriage today, they are agreed on one thing; that our 'morally liberated age' gives couples every chance to avoid a failed marriage. An extraordinary survey in America has overturned the new moralists. It proves that couples who married in the old-fashioned way – without much pre-marital physical contact – were just as happy and contented as 'modern' couples.
>
> Professor Martin Whyte, who led the research team in Detroit, said 'We have shown clearly that brides who took the opportunity to date other men or live with their partners before marriage have no better chance of a happy ending.'
>
> 'What really counts are the romantic feelings. The couple who felt romance had more chance of making a successful marriage.'

2

Read the article again.

a Which paragraphs answer these questions?
  1 What does Professor Whyte's survey prove?
  2 How important is romance?
b Answer the questions.

3

The article appeared in the *Daily Mail*. Choose the best headline for the article:

a *Old-fashioned love best, says professor*
b *American women prefer romance*
c *US survey backs romantic love*

4

Read the article *A triumph for romance*.

a Who speaks in the article – the husbands or the wives?
b Which couple were married in Didsbury?
c Where did Claire and Peter get engaged?
d When do couples celebrate their diamond wedding?

5

Read the article again. Compare the two women's . . . .

a feelings about being married
b knowledge of their husbands before marriage

6

Which woman . . . ?

a thinks that it's too easy to get out of marriage nowadays
b thinks it's a good thing to have other relationships before marriage
c thinks it's important to be able to talk to her husband about their differences

7

Work with a partner. Imagine that George meets Peter and they talk about their marriages. Think about what they would say to each other. Then act out their conversation.

Project

Organise a debate in your class.
The proposition to be debated is: We should be glad to live in a 'morally liberated' age.
You need to do the following things:

a *Choose four speakers, two in favour of the proposition and two against. One speaker from each side makes a speech which opens the debate; one speaker from each side closes the debate.*
b *Appoint a chairperson to control the debate.*
c *Decide how long each speaker may speak for.*
d *After the opening speeches, allow other members of the class to contribute to the debate.*
e *Take a vote at the end of the debate.*

A triumph for romance

First real kiss came on the wedding day

GEORGE and Agnes Sutton never held hands or kissed before they walked up the aisle at St Cuthbert's Church, Didsbury, on their wedding day in September 1930.

Sixty years later, they are about to celebrate their diamond wedding.

Their recipe for a successful marriage is simple. 'We get along very well and don't keep any differences going,' says George, now 88.

The couple met at work and courted for nine months before getting married.

Agnes had been out with 'one or two' boys before but she was George's first girlfriend.

For nine months, they met twice a week, and usually went to the pictures. But physical contact was out of the question.

'I don't think we ever held hands – I didn't know him properly,' said Agnes. 'He might have given me a peck on the cheek when he was leaving me, but we never held hands.'

Agnes says the key to their long, successful marriage has been their determination to sort out any differences.

'In our day, when you got married, that was it. There were marriages that didn't work out but you didn't leave your husband.

'Of course we have had rows. We've fallen out and not spoken to each other, but we have always managed to sort it out by sitting down and telling each other what we think,' she said.

'It's all too free and easy today. People are always switching, and changing. To me it doesn't seem right,' she said.

We'd both had time to make mistakes

FINANCIAL researcher Claire Randell, 28, married merchant banker Peter Bowman, 28, this March after a four-year courtship.

'I went to Durham University and had a couple of boyfriends there, then came to London for work. When I met Peter it wasn't love at first sight. He had had girlfriends before me, but neither of us was jealous about the past.

'In fact, I preferred that he had already had other relationships. We'd both had time to make mistakes, to know what we'd had and what we wanted. If you have been out with other people you recognise the goodness in a real relationship.

'Peter bought a flat near mine in West Hampstead, but after about two years we decided to buy a house together.

'The crunch came in our relationship when we went on a long trip. We went to India, Nepal, Hongkong and then Thailand, where Peter proposed on a palm-lined beach. I must admit I didn't have to think twice but just said yes.

'We didn't move back in together when we returned to London. I felt that if I was wearing white and having an old-fashioned wedding, I wanted to respect tradition by living apart at the end.

Different

'I'm really enjoying being married; it does feel different from just living together. With a woman there are obvious externals – the name change and the ring – but it's more than that. You feel you've made a big step. It's different and it's better,' said Claire.

Section C

1

Are these sentences true or false according to the factfile?

a British women are waiting longer before having children.

b Most children born to unmarried mothers live in one-parent families.

c There has been an enormous increase in the number of children living in one-parent families.

d Not many mothers with young children go out to work.

e Second marriages are much more stable than first marriages, because couples are older and more experienced.

2

Work with a partner. Discuss facts that interest you. In each case, how does the situation in your country compare with that in Britain?

Factfile | **Families**

1
The present population of Britain is 57 million. That is expected to rise to around 59 million by the year 2000 and 60 million by 2010.

2
The average number of children per family is 1.8.

3
The average age at which a woman has her first child is 27.3. In 1979 it was 26.7.

4
At birth the average life expectancy for British males is 72 years; for females it is 78.

5
More than 25% of British couples marrying now have lived together before marriage.

6
Twenty-seven per cent of all births are to unmarried mothers. More than half these babies are born to couples living together.

7
Twenty-five per cent of all households are one-person households. In 1961 the figure was 12%.

8
Fourteen per cent of British children live in one-parent families. In 1971 the figure was 7%.

9
Fifty-one per cent of all British women are in paid employment.

10
Two out of five women with pre-school age children (under 5 years) go out to work.

11
Britain has the highest divorce rate in European Community (EC) countries. It also has the highest marriage rate in the EC.

12
Two-thirds of second marriages in Britain end in divorce.

Festivals of faith

The number of Christians who go to church regularly has been falling, but for many the Christian faith is still part of life. How has the arrival of Islam and Hinduism in Britain affected the celebration of Christian festivals in some schools?

Section A

1

Complete the factfile with the figures given below.

- 300   80%   12%   1,000,000

2

Work with a partner.

a Discuss your figures.
b Check your answers on page 90.
c Do any of these facts surprise you?

Factfile | Religion

1
In 1990, 65% of the population of Britain described themselves as practising Christians.

2
By 2010 Christians are predicted to number 55% of the population.

3
In 1990 only .... of the population regularly attended a Christian church.

4
.... of couples who get married in Britain go through a religious ceremony.

5
The Bible is still a best-seller in Britain. Over a million copies are sold every year.

6
There are two official churches in Britain: the Church of England and the Church of Scotland. The Roman Catholic church also has members in both countries.

7
In 1970 there were about 300,000 Muslims in Britain: in 1990 this had risen to ....

8
There are more than .... mosques in Britain. The largest of these is in Central London.

9
The Jewish community in Britain numbers around 350,000.

10
There are also large Sikh and Hindu communities in Britain, each of which numbers around 300,000 members.

Section B

1

Work with a partner.

a What are the main religious festivals in your country?

b How are they celebrated?

2

Look at the two newspaper headlines.

a Do you think the two writers will put forward the same views?

b In what ways do you expect them to differ?

3

Read the first part of each of the two articles about Easter.

a Which article goes with which headline?

b Were the predictions you made in activity **2** correct?

Easter becomes Chocolate Sunday

Faith moves a mountain

WHATEVER happened to Easter? Like so many modern rituals, it seems hollowed out inside, a shadow of its former self. It used to be the great festival of death and rebirth in the European year. Now, to many, it seems to be little more than the day when you eat more chocolate than you should.

HE expected 20 people. 'It's Easter Day,' the vicar said. 'There will be a few more than usual.'

He sat watching the wind and the hail whip the Pembrokeshire mountains, working out what to tell them.

The Rev Anthony Bailey was in some hurry. There were four churches to look after and miles of mountain roads between them. 'I'll only get around to three of them,' he said, and even then the schedule was tight.

4

Read the rest of the article, *Faith moves a mountain*. Find out how many people attended the Easter service.

5

The writer of the article mentions a number of contrasts.

Complete these sentences.

a Only 20 people were expected at the Easter service, but ....

b In cathedrals people wore expensive clothes, but in St Mary's ....

c The roof of the church was rotting, but St Mary's ....

d In other places, archbishops spoke to the whole country, but in St Mary's ....
....

6

a Read the final paragraph again. What question did the writer ask? What was the vicar's reply?

b What reasons did people give for attending church on Easter Sunday?

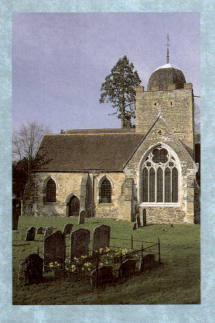

He could go to St Colman's in Llangolman, St Mary's in Maenclochog, and charge down to St Brynach's in Henry's Moat. He got all that in between 9 am and noon.

St Mary's might be the big one. Twenty people for Easter was what he expected. There were new lambs scattered on the hills. Lambs were the currency of the place. A farmer's family could spare an hour for church. Then it was back to the sheep.

'There is a lot of pressure at this time of year,' Anthony Bailey said. 'Twenty people may not seem much. It would make me happy.'

So why will there only be 20 in St Mary's, he was asked.

'Well, now, there are other pressures and many alternatives. In the past it was the thing to do. The country has become more materialistic in outlook.'

The vicar stood at the church door. A bell chimed its high note and the sound scattered rooks from their nests.

People hurried through the cold between old gravestones. The vicar had hoped for 20. Now it was 60 or 70 and he ran out of hymn books.

Pews filled and Anthony Bailey carried chairs through the church. People sat at the back and some had to stand. 'Unusual,' he whispered to himself, walking with his chairs and asking people to share the books.

A blind man tapped his white cane on the stone floor. Then he put his hand on the shoulder of the person in front of him and shuffled to a space in a pew.

On television there were pictures of cathedrals with people in fine clothes and fancy hats. In St Mary's in the mountains the women came bare-headed or with scarves on.

Children were pushed along by their parents and they sat in an annexe. Above them rot had attacked the wood of the roof. But St Mary's throbbed with the true spirit of Easter.

IN OTHER places Archbishops had on their snow-white vestments hung with the dazzle of gold, and they addressed nations. Here, a vicar talked to some farmers' families and was surrounded by a million sheep.

'It is the day we are all connected,' the vicar said, looking into friendly faces.

Pound coins fell onto the collection plate. Now everyone left the church. The Rev Bailey stood by the door and talked to them.

'All right, Eddie?' he said to the blind man. 'Yes, I feel a lot better today,' Eddie told him.

Women stopped and talked. Why did you come today, someone was asked. She said there was 'a plague of trouble in the world, people wanting and nobody giving'.

Another woman, a farmer's wife, paused, some children running into the graveyard ahead of her. 'I feel so worried about the way things are going in the country. It seems to be breaking up but the Church can help. That's why I came here today.'

'Happy Easter,' the vicar kept saying to his people.

'I don't always go to church,' someone else said. Then why did you come? 'That lady said it. You look at the way things are going, riots, evil, and, well . . . what's left if you don't have faith?'

The vicar dashed into the vestry and disrobed. He had to be in Henry's Moat in five minutes. The organ was already playing there.

Why did so many people turn up today? 'I really don't know,' he said, a little puzzled. 'I just do not know.' Then everybody went back to the mountains.

Section C

1

a Write down five words you associate with *Christmas*.

b Discuss with your partner what Christmas means to you. What do you like/dislike most about Christmas?

2

a Work with a partner. You are going to read a short poem called *Christmas* by Wendy Cope. Look at these words and decide . . . .

  1 which of them you would expect to find in the poem

  2 which of the words rhyme

  single cheerily dreadful families
  merry sing church tingle

b Now read the poem and see if you were right.

> At Christmas little children sing and merry
>   bells jingle
> The cold winter air makes our hands and faces
>   tingle
> And happy families go to church and cheerily
>   they mingle
> And the whole business is unbelievably
>   dreadful, if you're single.

3

Read the diary extract *Home for the holiday*.

a Whose week is described?

b Which festival does she talk about?

c What does she do at this time of year?

4

Read Joanna's diary again. Work with a partner. Would you like to spend Christmas doing something like Joanna? If so, what would you choose to do? If not, why not?

MY WEEK

Home for the holiday

Friday. Opening day. We start at 7 am with 150 volunteers putting up our eight televisions on the walls, arranging the mountains of assorted clothes and starting to peel vegetables for the evening meal. We will be serving pies, beans and fresh fruit at lunchtime.

□ □ □

Saturday. I would say that up to a quarter of those in the building this morning are under 25.

The reasons for their homelessness are diverse. Some have some kind of temporary roof over their heads but none has a permanent home.

□ □ □

Christmas Day. For the past 14 years, I have spent it in warehouses, bus garages, disused churches and halls. I would hate to spend it anywhere else. Certainly, the volunteers get as much out of it as anyone. I think we are better and fresher at our jobs because of it.

My only regret is that it means I spend Christmas away from my family, although I wouldn't be very good company if I spent the whole day at home. I go home for the evening to eat smoked salmon and open my presents. I even quite enjoy myself!

□ □ □

Wednesday. Today I feel exhausted. The thought crosses my mind that physically I may have met my upper limit.

But, it also comes into my mind that I *know* I can sleep in a bed every night of the year. So who am I to complain? I am glad I am where I am, doing what I can do.

Joanna Wade

The author, a solicitor, is vice-chair of Crisis *and an organiser of its annual* Open Christmas *for the homeless.*

Section D

1

Look at the photographs and the two captions below. Which caption accompanies which photograph?

a Decorations follow a strictly Christian theme at Kirkton Primary School in the Highlands.

b In multicultural celebrations at Islington Green Secondary School, pupils of all races give traditional performances and learn each other's national dances.

2

Read paragraphs 1–4 below. Match these summary sentences with the paragraphs.

a New ways of commemorating Christmas try to involve pupils of all religions.

b Insensitivity can damage relations between different communities.

c Parents and children seem to enjoy the new ways of commemorating Christmas.

d The celebration of Christmas in Britain is becoming more varied.

1
FROM small schools on remote Scottish islands to inner-city comprehensives catering for thousands, children are celebrating Christmas. The ways in which they do so, however, differ.

2
For many, the Nativity play and carol concert remain the tradition, but others are developing new customs and practices to ensure pupils from a range of backgrounds and faiths are included.

3
Lack of thought or sensitivity on the part of schools at Christmas could negate much of the hard work done throughout the year to improve community relations.

4
Parents seem to be satisfied with the diverse menu on offer. They are turning up in their thousands to see their offspring perform. What is certain is that for most children, celebrating Christmas is fun.

3

Match the statements below with the photographs on the previous page:

a 'Our children have the traditional Christmas story. They learn about the shepherds, the angels, and the Wise Men. I believe in it, that it really happened, and that makes it all the more exciting.'

b 'The traditional Christian Christmas celebration would be too narrow for a school like ours. We are trying to set Christmas in the context of other religious festivals. It is an important celebration of the multicultural nature of an international school and community.'

4

a Read the two articles on this page Find these words:
  fused   strands   friezes   exclusively
  fundamental

b Find synonyms for these words from the words in the box:

simple   mixed together   expensively   difficult
elements   only   posters   emotion   deviates

Captivated by the Bible Story

Annie MacDonald, headteacher of the tiny 11-pupil Kirkton Primary School in the Scottish Highlands, tells the Bible story in episodes to a captive audience of five-to nine-year-olds in the weeks leading up to Christmas. With her help, the children have charted the Holy Star's progress in friezes on the walls of their classroom, from the shepherds' hillside sighting of it to its resting place above the stable in Bethlehem.

By the end of this week, Miss MacDonald's final episode will bring the Wise Men to the foot of the crib for the climax of a story she says children still find exciting. Today, her pupils are taking part in a service conducted by the school chaplain, taking turns to read from the Bible and sing carols.

Kirkton, which serves the rural community of Bunchrew, near Inverness, concentrates exclusively on the Christian account of Jesus's birth because that "is what Christmas is all about".

That approach would be too fundamental for some schools, but with the children sharing a broadly Protestant background, Miss MacDonald can be confident of parental support.

Festivities that bring together a world of different traditions

IRISH, Greek, Bengali and West Indian culture fused in a "One World" celebration of Christmas at Islington Green Secondary School, north London.

More than 700 parents, many standing, crowded into the school hall to watch the strands of their many different cultures and faiths threaded together in music and dance.

Here, the study of Christmas strays well beyond the crib. Ms Jeffery says

"My first-year pupils look at Christmas in its social and historical context. We examine how the Victorians invented the family Christmas and practices such as sending cards."

The children also learn who do and do not celebrate Christmas. "It is particularly important for them to understand each other; so much of prejudice is based on ignorance," she says.

5

In groups discuss how religious festivals are celebrated in your country.

Project

Work in a group to investigate attitudes to religious festivals.

a *Draw up a questionnaire on attitudes to Christmas or any other religious festival in your country.*

b *Ask a group of young people and a group of adults to complete the questionnaire.*

c *Look at the results. Do the two groups respond in the same way? What differences are there in their responses?*

A nation of immigrants

The people of Britain are black, brown, and white. They have always come from a variety of origins. Now the multi-cultural nature of today's Britain is being celebrated more and more. But racism still exists.

Section A

Two wedding breakfasts for TV-am newsgirl

By RICHARD MIDDLETON

THIS IS the private side of TV newsgirl Lisa Aziz that the viewers haven't seen.

The 26-year-old breakfast show presenter wore a traditional sari for a Moslem ceremony to bless her register office wedding held a fortnight ago.

Lisa, who returned to the TV-am newsdesk today, wanted her husband – millionaire Dutch broker Frank Ter Voorde – to be initiated in her faith. The ceremony followed a honeymoon and trip to Holland to celebrate with the groom's family.

'Having my marriage blessed was very important to me,' said Lisa, who earns £75,000 a year for her part in Good Morning Britain's ratings success.

'And it was a good way of introducing Frank properly into the Moslem community. We celebrate with a feast, soft drinks and traditional music.'

Lisa, who was voted Asian of the Year in 1989, hosted a party at her parents' South London home after the blessing.

Her father is from Bangladesh and her mother is English, and the guests reflected the international flavour by flying in from India and America.

The couple's Moslem ceremony

Lisa and Frank at the register office

1
Work with a partner. Look at the two photographs and compare how the couple look.

2
Read the article
a Who is the *TV-am* newsgirl?
b Why did she have two wedding ceremonies?

3
Read the article again. Find two reasons why Lisa wanted to have her marriage blessed.

4
What does the article tell you about Lisa's job, religion, family and age. Why does the article tell us more about Lisa than about Frank?

Section B

1
a What do you understand by the word *immigrants*?
b Read the article. Where have immigrants to Britain come from?

2
Read the article again. Match these headings with the correct paragraphs.

a Widespread influence
b Discrimination
c Immigration not new
d Refugees from persecution
e Citizens of the old Empire

3
Which immigrant groups came to Britain . . . ?
a in the 1930s
b in the 1940s

4
Which word would you use to describe John Barnes' attitude to racial abuse?

brave   cowardly   sensible
tolerant   relaxed

5
a Write a title for the whole article.
b Work in a group. Compare your titles. Choose the best title.

6
Work in a group. Is there racial discrimination in your country? Why do you think this kind of discrimination still exists?

People have been migrating to Britain for centuries. Immigrants have come to Britain from all parts of the world. Some came to avoid political or religious persecution, others to find a better way of life or to escape from poverty. Others still came to join members of their family who had already settled in Britain.

Many of these immigrants were refugees. In the 1930s Jews fled persecution in other parts of Europe to settle in Britain. After the end of the Second World War many citizens of Eastern European countries decided to stay in Britain. More recently refugees have come from as far afield as Uganda, Chile, Iran, and Sri Lanka.

Another group of immigrants were the citizens of the former British Empire. In the 1940s and 50s, people from the West Indies came to find work in Britain. Later, immigrants from Cyprus, India, Pakistan, Hong Kong and Bangladesh arrived, each bringing their own distinctive language, culture and religion to this country.

Now the children and grand-children of this last group of immigrants have grown up and taken their places in a multicultural Britain. More than 2½ million strong, black Britons tend to be concentrated in particular areas of inner cities but their influence extends well beyond the big cities. Black Britons are well represented in sport and the media and there are few small towns in Britain that don't have an Indian or a Chinese restaurant and a Pakistani-owned post office or grocery.

Although racial discrimination was outlawed by the Race Relations act of 1976, it does still occur – sometimes subtly, sometimes not so subtly. Black footballers, for example, are sometimes subjected to racial taunts from supporters of opposing teams. How do they feel about it? John Barnes, one of England's leading black footballers, shrugs his shoulders. 'If you let these people get to you,' he says, 'then they've won. I just ignore them and try to play even better.'

Section C

1

Read the article. Is it about
… ?

a how black people are
presented on British
television
b how few black presenters
there are on television
c plans to increase the
number of black people on
television

2

Read the article again and
answer these questions:

a What is Cherry Ehrlich's
job?
b What percentage of BBC
staff are non-white?
c How do we know that
progress is being made in
appointing black reporters?

3

If you had a photo of Cherry
Ehrlich, what would you write
as a caption?

4

Write a headline for the
article.

Cherry Ehrlich was appointed the BBC's first Equal Opportunities Officer in 1986. She is worried ethnic minorities regard the BBC as a closed world: "If people can't see people like them in a particular industry then they think that it's not for them."

Figures for last year show that 94 per cent of BBC staff were of European origin and only six per cent of ethnic origin, many of whom were in low-grade jobs.

"We don't think 6 per cent is good enough," says Ms Ehrlich. Many of her plans are already in action – training schemes aimed exclusively at ethnic minorities, and employment targets for directors to reach in order to change the situation.

"The aim is to get black reporters and producers through faster," she says.

"If they took the conventional route it would take much longer. We really do want a broad range of candidates and the excellent response rate to these schemes shows that we just hadn't been getting the message across before.

"We are seeing increases in the numbers of ethnic minorities at the BBC," she says, "Two years ago I would have known the names of all the non-European presenters and reporters here – now there's so much going on I can hardly remember any!

5

Read these profiles of two black television presenters and complete the biographical tables.

	Raj Dhanda	Trevor MacDonald
age/year born	....	....
place of birth	....	....
nationality	....	....
present job	....	....

6

What do the two men say about race and colour? How do their opinions differ? In what ways are they the same?

Not just a token – Trevor MacDonald

TREVOR MACDONALD, co-presenter of ITN's News at Ten, was born in Trinidad, Jamaica. He joined the BBC in London in 1969 when he was 30 and is now a familiar television face, but still one of only a few black national news readers.

"The other day a man said to me 'Of course, you're only there because you're black.' It stung me but it didn't hurt me. It only made me more determined to be better than everyone else."

Hard work is his motto and he's proud of being a hard working West Indian. "At the BBC they don't care what colour you are – they just want you to get the facts down in a good, hard way."

He is philosophical about ethnic minority representation in the media: "Things are definitely improving, but a lot more hard work needs to be done. These things will always take time to become the norm."

More Scottish than anything – Raj Dhanda

RAJ DHANDA works as a presenter on the BBC's Clothes Show. He is followed around by groups of adoring females when he does his shopping at the weekend.

He was born and brought up in Glasgow and studied at Glasgow University. "I hate being categorised, but I very loosely call myself black. The term 'Asian' makes it sound as if people have just arrived. I'm British. In fact I'm more Scottish than anything.

"I have the best of both worlds and make the best of both of them." He has started a group at the BBC called the Black Workers Group. Racial prejudice is not something Dhanda has ever experienced in his work. "If you are good and capable, you'll get on in whatever field you choose."

As to the future, he is uncertain except that he would like to do another Clothes Show series, and at 24 he has years ahead of him.

7
Look at the table on ethnic groups in Britain and complete the factfile.

Ethnic groups in Britain

Ethnic group	Percentage of ethnic population 1981	Estimated population (thousands) 1986-88	Estimated Percentage 1986-88		Change in population	
			of ethnic population	of total population	1981 Thousands	1986/88 %
West Indian	25	495	19	0.9	− 33	− 6
Indian	35	787	31	1.4	+ 59	+ 8
Pakistani	14	428	17	0.8	+144	+ 51
Bangladeshi	2	108	4	0.2	+ 56	+109
Mixed	10	287	11	0.5	+ 70	+ 32
All ethnic minority groups	100	2,577	100	4.7	+485	+ 23
White	—	51,470	—	94.4	+470	+ 1

*F*actfile | Minorities

1
During the 1980s the ethnic minority population rose by ....

2
The number of Britons of West Indian origin fell by ....

3
The ethnic minority group which showed the biggest increase in numbers was the ....

4
But the group which showed the biggest percentage increase was the ....

5
The white population grew by ....

6
There was also a big increase in numbers of people of mixed race. Their numbers rose by ....

*P*roject

Work.in a group. Think of a minority in your country which suffers discrimination. This minority may be discriminated against because of their race, their nationality, or their physical or mental capabilities. Plan a campaign to make the general public more aware of the ways in which this group is discriminated against. Some possible activities include:

a a demonstration
b organise a letter-writing campaign to your local newspaper or radio/TV station
c design a badge and/or T-shirt for supporters of your campaign
d think up a slogan
e write a leaflet that sets out the facts of the case

Remember that your aim is to persuade people who may not yet share your views to change their minds about this issue.

Answer Key

Unit 1   *page 2*

Section A

2 Profile 1   Queen Elizabeth II
Profile 2   Prince Charles, the Prince of Wales
Profile 3   Prince Philip, the Duke of Edinburgh
Profile 4   Princess Anne, the Princess Royal

3a the Trooping of the Colour for the Queen's
birthday and the Investiture of Prince Charles
when he became Prince of Wales in 1969
 b the Save the Children Fund and the Duke of
Edinburgh Award Scheme

4a the two royals described are Prince Andrew, the
Duke of York, and Queen Elizabeth the Queen
Mother

Section B

2a Prince Charles was at Stratford's Swan Theatre
and Princess Diana was at a London conference on
children with Aids.
 b Prince Charles was speaking to academics and
Princess Diana was speaking to health
professionals and volunteers.
 c Prince Charles was speaking about progressive
teaching methods and Princess Diana about how
to treat children who have Aids.

Section C

Factfile
1   State, Government   2   1953   3   William
4   Andrew, Edward   5   1926, June   6   million
7   visits   8   Andrew, helicopter   9   Charles
10   1937, Edward VIII

Unit 2   *page 7*

Section A

Factfile
1   b   2   The House of Lords   3   c (There are
630 MPs)   4   b (7% of the MPs are women at time
of printing)   5   b   6   a   7   c   8   b
9   c   10   b   11   c   12   c, e and f

Section B

1c serious political business: para's 2, 3 and 4
pageantry: the last 4 para's.
2a the Prime Minister
 b the Queen
 c the Governments views
 d in the House of Lords
 e members of the royal family, Lords, and MPs
 f Wednesday
 g November

 h 11.00 in the morning

3   7, 4, 2, 3, 6, 8, 1, 5

Section C

3 The word 'lost' is used because the women never
quite made it to become Labour MP's and have
now come out of politics. 'Lost' means that Labour
has lost them as potential candidates.

4a the Labour Party
 b yes
 c yes, Patricia Hewitt: she stood for Leicester East
but was not successful

5a all three articles refer directly or indirectly to the
long hours worked by MPs
 b the profile about Mary Kaldor mentions being
shortlisted and attending 'masses of meetings' and
the Patricia Hewitt profile mentions being 'chosen'
to fight a seat
 c the Margaret Hodge profile mentions how she
would 'love to be part of a Labour government
influencing change'
 d Mary Kaldor says that she has enjoyed working in
the peace movement in a way she couldn't have
done as an MP

Unit 3   *page 12*

Section A

2

date	population
1800	1 billion
1975	2 billion
2030	10.2 billion

3 disgorging noxious gases into the atmosphere,
dumping toxic waste into rivers and oceans,
tearing up the countryside to accommodate our
rubbish

4 rise in temperatures and sea levels – flooding,
infertile land and water contamination

5a if we act now we can do something to turn things
around and save the planet – it is not too late
 b because we are annihilating our world which in
turn will lead to our own destruction

6   habitat/environment   equilibrium/balance
toxic/poisonous   project/predict
drive up/increase   tracts/areas
spurred/motivated   ill-advised/badly-thought out

9 recycle things – don't just use them once

Section B

2 the article which starts 'Evidence is mounting . . .' because this article states that a study has been sponsored by Lancashire County Council (3rd paragraph) and the other one refers to it having been published that day (2nd paragraph)

4a false (evidence is mounting that townspeople are at risk from illnesses linked to sewage pollution of the sea, even if they do not swim in it)
 b false (Lancashire County Council sponsored Lancaster University to carry out the study)
 c true
 d true
 e false (headaches are not mentioned in the text, although fever and sinusitis are mentioned and this could cause headaches)
 f true (although Dr. Lucking does not actually use the words 'pollution-related illnesses'. He does however imply that this is what he means when he says 'It is unacceptable that this is going on on our doorstep')

5b John Hall – 'This is seriously going to affect . . .'
 Louise Ellman – 'The water authority's proposals . . .'
 Dr. Martin Lucking – 'We have known . . .'

Section C

1 Heritage Coasts are coastal areas in England and Wales, protected from development.

2 England, Wales, Scotland
 National Trust, Countryside Commission

Unit 4   *page 17*

Section A

2a 2, 3
 b 2   1949   3   10

3a 1

4a protection for the countryside, provide opportunity for people to enjoy them
 b possible answer: if allowing tourists to visit a place causes erosion e.g. a mountain peak or path

5 north-west, approximately 45–50, 14 million

6a b or c

7a 1   Hawkshead   3   Scafell Pike
   2   Windermere   4   Skiddaw

Section B

4 Donald Angus – park ranger
 Anne Barnett – housewife and owns bike hire business
 Neil Allinson – an upland access adviser for the National Trust
 Eddie Hibbert – Secretary of the Lake District Ramblers' Association

Section C

1a William Wordsworth
 b Dorothy

2a she writes as if the daffodils were alive
 b 1   yes   2   a crowd   3   a cloud

3b cloud/crowd   hills/daffodils   trees/breeze
   shine/line   way/bay   glance/dance
   pattern: ab ab cc
   it is the same in both verses

Unit 5   *page 22*

Section A

2a *Comic Relief* is a fund raising organisation
 Red Nose Day is the main fund day for *Comic Relief* where people invent humorous ways of raising money
 Charity Projects is the head office for *Comic Relief*
 b selling red noses, people are sponsored to do ridiculous and amusing things
 c putting jelly in their underpants, sitting in a bath of custard or baked beans etc.
 d aim: to let people know what happens to their money
 e good: man in Kenya who has been taught to perform cataract operations
   bad: Richardson saying 'Enjoy your supper' to viewers while thin Africans are eating from small bowls of grain and nuts
   why?: because they don't try to make people feel guilty
 f guilt, spending money on emergency relief, depicting the needy in a patronising way

3b to show that although this is humorous charity work, it is taken very seriously as peoples' lives are involved
 c *Comic Relief* have designed new noses that will be hard to pirate. This should halt the black market on red noses.

Section B

1a 1   true   2   true   3   true

3a Jane Tewson
 b director of *Red Nose Day*
 c as a diary

4a Malawi, to assess refugee needs
b 1 people who have had to leave their homes for political, religious or economic reasons
2 at least 800,000 from Mozambique

5a Fiona
b 1 Monday   2 Thursday   3 Sunday
4 Wednesday   5 Friday

6a on the right: forested land, on the left: huts
b Jane: because it is so hot with mosquitoes humming
Rob: because it is a cooler night in comparison with others
c because she walks on her elbows
d to show how little they earn
e because people often get upset stomachs when they first arrive in Malawi
f she was worrying about Fiona in hospital with cerebral malaria
g the woman thinks that having children is very important (perhaps so that they can look after you in your old age) but Jane perhaps feels sorry for her because she has had so many children in her short life and in such poor conditions that 5 of them have died

7 a at the crack of dawn   b fancy
c bowled over   d hardened
e my heart stops

Section C
Factfile
2 1,500
3 27
4 41
5 82
6 17

Unit 6   *page 27*

Section A

2a 1 'Sachs' unspeakable thoughts'
2 'There's no need . . .'
b TV viewers, businessmen

3a he could speak no English when he came to England as a boy
b Manuel, the Spanish waiter in BBC's *Fawlty Towers*
c *Lingo*

4a 'peeved': to be annoyed
'beleaguered': experiencing a lot of difficulties, opposition or criticism

b he was peeved because he didn't think he *was* little but that was the only sentence he could say
he was beleaguered because Basil Fawlty, the hotel owner, treated him so badly

5c they use Spanish to show how irritating it is not to understand a language – 'In the single market everyone speaks various languages'
d 3

Section B

1a Roy
b Suzi
c Roy
d Suzi
e Suzi

2 Suzi's text: *We can link up in a spirit of peace*
Roy's text: *Brussels could teach us a lot*

Unit 7   *page 32*

Section A

2 200, 2, dictionary, 21, Christmas, child, 8.6, 6.7, crime, 75%

Section B

1b an agreement   a deal
consequently   as a result
recovered   recouped
overseas sales   exports
spectacularly   dramatically
moved   transferred

2a Books are big business: 62,000 books annually, value of exports £660 million in 1987, Jeffrey Archer signed to Harper Collins 1990 for £11 million and Ken Follett to Dell for £7 million
b 1991 the book trade in trouble: sales down, job losses
c other problems: the six figure sums paid out on author 'transfer' deals not recouped through sales

3 three, However, twice, because, promotion, hand, profit

Section C

1

event	date
born	1921
first job	1937
married	1941
first book	1962
husband died	1964

2 crime

3b a3 b4 c1 d5 e6 f2

4a locked the door, stuck tape across the window sill
b intruders
c a blow from a fist or a stick
d down a well
e 'walk' up the side (the well is only 3 feet in diameter and she can put her feet against one side and her back against the other and 'work her way upwards')

5a 1 at the very end of the extract (d) 'She had always been a survivor. She would survive'
2 when she is down the well – (extract d) 'She wouldn't let herself drown, wouldn't die in this horrible place'
3 when she first hits the water at the bottom of the well (extract d) 'Desperately she trod water, . . . Frantically moving hands and feet . . .'

Section D

2a couldn't make head nor tail of it
b off by heart
c train of thought
d without any argument

Unit 8   *page 37*

Section A

2 doing speaking exercises together

3 to give her more confidence and to present a better image of the hotel

4a paragraph 2
b paragraph 3
c paragraph 4
d paragraph 1

5a four-star   excellent
b reburbishment   improvement
c diagnosed   discovered

6 he is socio-linguist and teacher of English at Kumamoto University in Japan. His book is called *Does Accent Matter?*
7a all of them

Section B

1 because it has been influenced by many different languages over the years

2 Celts   500 BC
Romans   55 BC

Angles and Saxons   700 AD

3 the up-and-coming middle classes, in order to be successful (get on) in society, Middle English was formed (combination of Old English and French)

4a People who lived in different parts of the country spoke English in their own way, often using different words to describe things and different sentence structures
b English became standardised

5a radar, laser, punk, heavy metal, house music

Section C

2 Gaelic

3a banned   proscribed
b remains   remnant
c mass   concentration
d strongholds   redoubts
e lost its strength languished
f invented   improvised

4

	then	now
Celtic culture	glorious, stretching across Europe, ballads, art, keeping Christianity alive	dying out, poor teaching materials, just a few people left
Gaelic language	extensively spoken	only 473 children under 5 speak it, until recently it was banned and children were beaten
Skye	was the heartland of the Gaels	the only concentration of speakers live on the Staffin Peninsula

5 because there are so few people left now and very few speak the language.

Unit 9   *page 42*

Section A

Factfile
1 a, 2 c, 3 a, 4 a, e, f, 5 b, c, e, 6 a
7 a

Section B

1 teachers are complaining about the amount of extra administration they have to do

3a paragraph 2
 b paragraph 3
 c paragraph 4

4a true
 b false
 c false
 d true
 e false
 f false

Section C

1   GCSE passes
                              ↓
                         A levels
              University ╱   ╲ Polytechnic

2a Work: a job with some training   Education: retake
   GCSE's, a youth training qualification, or a BTEC
   diploma
 b Work
 c sixth form college

Unit 10   *page 46*

Section A

Factfile
1 27.1 million,   2   11.3%
3 £4,524   4   43%   5   43.5 hours
6 29.8 hours   7   1935   8   1990

Section B

3a 3
 b Paul 16,   Carl 17,   Karen 16
 c taken GCSE exams

Section C

1a people who are looking for a job
 b Department of Employment

2 personal confidence, the ability to present yourself
   to others, and a knowledge of the local job market,
   persuading an employer that you've got the skills
   and knowledge needed for the job, being positive
   about yourself

5 leaves school, works in office, does A-level course,
   completes course at North London Polytechnic,
   becomes self-employed photographer

6a encouraged her that her photographs were good
 b put her in touch with the enterprise team at South

Thames Training and Enterprise Council
 c gave her an enterprise allowance of £40 per week
   to help her get started
 d let her assist them so that she could learn

7 advantages: offered challenge and variety
   disadvantages: no paid holidays or sick leave

8 run a business   a
   deal with customers   a
   get commissions for magazines   b
   photograph record covers   b
   build up the business   b
   work with other photographers   a

Section D

2 he makes furniture out of wood – a cabinet maker

3 a person's identity is not defined by their job

4a 2

Unit 11   *page 51*

Section A

1a The Times
 b The Sun
 c The Daily Mail

3a *The Times, The Sun, The Independent, The
   Guardian, The Daily Mail, The Mirror*
 b quality newspapers: *The Times, The Independent,
   The Guardian*
   tabloids: *The Mirror, The Sun*

4a very keen   voracious
   shows   reflects
   very important   crucial
   unimportant news   trivia

Section B

1a 'The couch-potato . . .' article
 b 'It is possible . . .' article
 c 'The couch-potato . . .' article

2a 5
 b pets
 c 33%
 d declining
 e 25
 f Britain

Section C

1a a magazine, a window-cleaning fluid

Section D

Factfile
1a   9,   1b   2,   1c   12,   1d   3,   1e   11

3a 24
 b sport, business, science and technology, music, drama, religion and light entertainment

Unit 12   *page 55*

Section B

1   they are a series of approximately 50 concerts held every year.

2   The word 'Proms' is short for 'Promenade', meaning 'walk'. This refers back to the original Proms concerts when people were allowed to stand and even walk around during the concert.

3a Sir Henry Wood: conducted the first Promenade Concert in London in 1894
 b Andrew Davis: conducted his first Last Night of the Proms in 1988
 c Sir Edward Elgar: wrote 'Pomp and Circumstance' in 1902, traditionally played at the 'Last Night' every year

4a Land of Hope and Glory
 b 1 Britain, the 'land', our 'Mother'
   2 our country's values should spread all over the world

6a more

7   'the massed middle classes', 'younger than other concert audiences with a larger proportion aged under 25 and a smaller one over 44', 'They are also more male', 'one in five had been to a pop concert in the previous year and one in two to opera', 'Most came because of the programme or "because it was a Prom"', 5% for the orchestra, and 4% for the conductor'

Section C

1a 'Sample Nigel's string fever'
 b 'Kennedy lifts a damp audience'
 c 'Sample Nigel's string fever'
 d 'Kennedy lifts . . .' is a newspaper report about the concert advertised in 'Sample Nigel's string fever'

3a 1 Sunday August 19th,   2 6.30pm (but gates open at 4.30pm),   3 Crystal Palace Bowl in south-east

London,   4 £16, £55   5 Bruch concerto and *The Four Seasons*,   6 25,000

4a fairly heavy rain falling for short periods of time, often falling between periods of sunshine
 b the individual spots of rain
 c loud crashes heard during an electric storm
 d rained very heavily – the water falls as though being tipped out of a bucket
 e slightly wet

Unit 13   *page 60*

Section B

1   it reflects the taste of one man, Sir William Burrell

Section C

1a yes, brothers and sisters
 b about fifty years ago

3   similarities: not born in Scotland, moved to Glasgow in youth, studied at Glasgow School of Art, died in middle age

7   part 1, b
   part 2, c
   part 3, d
   part 4, a

8   perhaps the dark and gloomy things are comfortable because they are familiar and because people are fond of things of the past

9a rubble, chill, dying, fell coldly to the ground, islands of stone
 b left standing, life, shrill, children, jump

Unit 14   *page 64*

Section A

1a Glen Affric, Scotland
 b Deptford
 c Forest Hill, SE23
 d Glen Affric, Scotland
 e West Wimbledon
 f South Cambridgeshire
 g Glen Affric, Scotland
 h Forest Hill SE23

2   £15,000, 20 months, it has dropped by £10,000 from the original asking price

3a its position 'You can see the common; there are masses of restaurants and it's only 10 minutes walk to the railway station.'

c 2: the people who are buying have lots of properties to choose from and prices are low, so they can take their time

d she still believes someone will like it and want to buy it.

Factfile

5 195,000, 150,000, 66%, £62,000, 72%, 7%

Section B

1a out on the streets

b asking people for money

Section C

3a arguments and splits between families and with friends

b problems with landlord/lady, cannot pay the mortgage

c landlord/lady owns property which he or she does not live in, it is rented out to a tenant but owner-occupier lives in their own property.

d people who fall behind on their mortgage payments

4 Brian: family/friends falling out
Malcolm: partners separating, cannot pay the mortgage ('I got into debt')
Cathy: families/friends falling out

Unit 15   *page 69*

Section A

2a at least 7: mother, father, sister, brother and the writer as well as the 'kids' referred to in verse 1 and 3 (this word is plural so there are at least 2 kids)

b mother

c brother 'he can't hang around'

3b A person who is house proud literally has pride in his/her house. He or she keeps it very clean, neat and tidy. It always looks nice.

4a Father gets up late for work
Mother has to iron his shirt.
Then she sends the kids to school
Sees them off with a small kiss.
She's the one they're going to miss
In lots of ways.

Section B

1a Professor Martin Whyte led the research team

b because his research team produced some interesting results.

2a 1 paragraph 2   2 paragraph 3

b 1 it 'proves that couples who married in the old-fashioned way – without much pre-marital physical contact – were just as happy and contented as modern couples'
2 it is very important – it is 'what really counts', 'the couple who felt romance had more chance of making a successful marriage'

4a mainly the wives

b George and Agnes

c on a beach in Thailand

d after 60 years of marriage

5a Agnes: marriage is for life, the important thing is to sort out your problems and differences by talking things through, you mustn't give up too easily
Claire: marriage is different to living together, it feels better

b Agnes: they saw each other twice a week for nine months before they got engaged, they did not hold hands or have any physical contact except possibly the occasional quick kiss on the cheek, Agnes didn't even know how babies were born
Claire: lived with Peter for a while before they decided to get married, after a four year courtship and a world trip.

6a Agnes

b Claire

c Agnes

Section C

Factfile

1a true	1b false	1c true	1d true
1e false			

Unit 16   *page 73*

Section A

Factfile

3 12%   **4** 80%   **7** 1,000,000   **8** 300

Section B

2a they will put forward different views

b 'Faith moves a mountain' means that someone has great faith, but 'Easter becomes Chocolate Sunday' means that to most people there is very little true religious meaning to Easter

3a 'Easter becomes Chocolate Sunday' . . . 'Whatever happened to Easter?'
'Faith moves a mountain' . . . 'He expected 20 people. . .'

4 60 or 70

5a 60 or 70 came and he ran out of hymn books.
 b the women came bare-headed or with scarves on.
 c throbbed with the spirit of Easter.
 d a vicar talked to some farmers' families and was surrounded by a million sheep.

6a 'Why did so many people turn up?'
 'I really don't know.'
 b the world was in such a mess that it was bringing them back to God – their faith was suddenly very important to them

Section C

2a 2 single/tingle/sing   cheerily/merry/families

3a Joanna Wade: a solicitor
 b Christmas
 c she helps to organise the annual *Open Christmas* for the homeless which gives food and shelter for homeless people at Christmas

Section D

2a 2
 b 3
 c 4
 d 1

4 fused   mixed together
  strands   elements
  friezes   posters
  exclusively   only
  fundamental simple

Alternative Project
Work in a group to produce a magazine/newspaper advertisement to attract tourists to attend a religious ceremony or visit a religious site in your country. Include an illustration, a slogan and a short text.

Unit 17   *page 79*

Section A

2a Lisa Aziz
 b because she is of mixed ethnic origins – her father is a Moslem from Bangladesh and her mother is English.

3 to introduce her husband to the Moslem community and to initiate him into the Moslem faith

4 Lisa is a news reader on breakfast television and earns £75,000 a year. She is a Moslem like her father and she was 26 at the time of the wedding. We are not told much about Frank because he is not famous and the public would not be as interested in him as in Lisa.

Section B

1a immigrants are people who move from their country of origin to another country and live and settle there taking that country's nationality
 b Jews, people from Eastern Europe, Uganda, Chile, Iran, Sri Lanka, West Indies, Cyprus, India, Pakistan, Hong Kong and Bangladesh

2a paragraph 4
 b paragraph 5
 c paragraph 1
 d paragraph 2
 e paragraph 3

3a Jews
 b Eastern Europeans, West Indians

Section C

1 plans to increase the number of black people on television

2a Equal Opportunities Officer for the BBC
 b 6% (at time of printing)
 c she can't name many of the non-European presenters and reporters because there are now so many

5

	Raj Dhanda	Trevor MacDonald
age	24	born 1939
place of birth	Glasgow, Scotland	Trinidad, Jamaica
present job	BBC Clothes Show Presenter	Co-presenter of News at Ten on Independent Television News

Factfile
7 1 23%   2 6%   3 Pakistanis
  4 Bangladeshis   5 1% (470,000)
  6 32% (70,000)

Heinemann International
A division of Heinemann Publishers (Oxford) Ltd.,
Halley Court, Jordan Hill, Oxford, OX2 8EJ

OXFORD LONDON EDINBURGH
MADRID ATHENS BOLOGNA PARIS
MELBOURNE SYDNEY AUCKLAND SINGAPORE TOKYO
IBADAN NAIROBI HARARE GABORONE

ISBN 0 435 28038 4

Designed by Bob Wheeler
Cover illustration by Chris Wadden and Moggy
Illustrations by Rowan Barnes-Murphy, Jerry Collins,
Deborah Gyan, Amanda Hutt, Clyde Pearson, Joe Wright

Photo research by Anne Lyons and Suzanne Williams
Commissioned photographs by Paul Freestone
Typeset by Wyvern Typesetting Ltd., Bristol
Other typesetting by Scan Graphic
Printed and bound in Spain, at Mateu Cromo

Author Acknowledgements

The author would like to thank participants and colleagues on the
following courses and seminars for their helpful comments on the
sections of this book during the course of its development: Russian
teachers' conversion course, Bratislava 1990; Austrian AMS teachers'
seminar, Raach 1992 (especially Pat Häusler); Bell College, Saffron
Walden, 1991–2; TESOL Summer Institute, Bratislava 1992.

Karen Jacobs has worked indefatigably to refine and focus the
manuscript. I am grateful for the many fresh insights she has provided.

I owe a very special debt of thanks to Liz Driscoll, a constant source of
inspiration as editor, teacher, and writer whose support for this project
from concept to completion has been matchless.

Alan C McLean
September 1992

Acknowledgements

The publishers would like to thank the following for kind permission to
use their material in this book:

Stan Abbott/The Independent text adapted from *Child bathers face health
risk*, p14; The Advertising Standards Authority for complaint text, p53; H
Bauer Publishing for *Sachs' unspeakable thoughts*, p28; Spencer
Bright/Solo Syndication for *Kennedy lifts a damp audience*, p59; The
British Broadcasting Corporation for *BBC World Service 1990*, and
Languages and Hours, p54; BBC Proms 92 for *Five things we ask you not
to do at the Proms* (programme), p56, and extract from *Prom 90*
programme (Andrew Davies quotation), p57; The Body Shop for *No time
to waste*, p12, and logo p13; Maggie Brown/The Independent for
Television viewing down by 5 per cent, p52, and *Reading remains popular
despite lure of television*, p32; Carcanet Press Limited/Edwin Morgan *To
Joan Eardley* from *Collected Poems*, p63; Roy Clementson/The
Independent for text, p30; Consumers' Association, Limited for *Heritage
Coasts* from *Holiday Which?* January 1985, p16; Ngaio Crequer/The
Independent for *Pace of change sows the seeds of disillusion*, p43;
William Dalrymple/The Independent Magazine for *The last day of the
Gaels*, p41; Department of Employment (Crown Copyright) for *The
Confidence Factor*, p48 & 49; Education Guardian for *How the money
gets to Africa*, p24, and *Why homeless?*, p67; Cherry Ehrlich/The
Independent for text on equal opportunities at the BBC, p81; Faber &
Faber Limited for: Wendy Cope, *A Christmas Poem* from *Drinking Cocoa
with Kingsley Amis*, p76, TS Eliot, *Burnt Norton*, p36, and PD James, *An
Unsuitable Job For A Woman*, p35; The Guardian for: *Couch Potato* text,
p52, *The European Community* (EC) and *Who we send to the European
Community* graphics, p31, *The right royal State Opening of Parliament*,
p8, and the *Women in Government* table, p10; Nicky Hughes/
Independent on Sunday for *Victorian charm*, p64; Amanda Hutt
(artwork), p72; IMP for *Our House* lyrics by Madness, p69; The
Independent for: *Did you make the grades*, p44, *Festivities that bring
together a world of different traditions*, and *Captivated by the Bible Story*,
p78, *Hot off the press*, p39, *More Scottish than anything* – Raj Dhanda,
and *Not just a token* – Trevor MacDonald p82, *How here is the news*,
adapted, p39, profiles on PD James and Sally Beauman, p33, text on PD
James, p34, property descriptions, p64, *Teacher training wastage in the
1980's*, p43, *The dawn of English*, p39, and for *1066 and all that*, p39; The
Independent Magazine for *proms* illustration, p57; William Leith/The
Independent for *The hard-nosed business of Red Nose Day*, p22; Robert
Maycock/The Independent for *Proms ride a wave of classical popularity*,
p58; Richard Middleton/Solo Syndication for *Two wedding breakfasts for
TV-AM newsgirl*, p79; Michael O'Mara Books, for *The Royal Family Tree*,
p2; New Statesman & Society for *Labour's Lost MP's* text, p10; The
Observer for *Easter becomes Chocolate Sunday*, p74; Tony Parker/Martin
Secker and Warburg Limited for *Life After Life*, p36; Malcolm
Pithers/The Independent for text adapted from *A welcome in the hillsides
for considerate bike-riders*, p20; Rosalind Sharpe/The Independent for *It
ain't what you say* ..., p37 & 38; Solo Syndication for: *A triumph for
romance*, p70 & 71, *Ethnic Group table*, p83, *Faith moves a mountain*,
p75, *In their words*, p47, *Sample Nigel's string fever*, p59, and *Stand up to
the trendies*, p5; Suzi Stembridge/The Independent for text, p30; The
Stapleford Partnership, Wilton, Wilts for extract and tables from
Thatcher's Children, p47; Struthers Creations Ltd/The Hargreaves
Organisation for *Glasgow's Miles Better*, p60; Jane Tewson/The
Independent for *Axes drawn in the mud* (adapted), p25; Joanna
Wade/The Independent for *My Week, Home for the holiday*, p76; Joe
Wright for illustration, p28.

Photographic Acknowledgements

Mrs P Black/George Oliver (Joan Eardley, p. 63); BBC (p. 28), (Alex von
Koettlitz, p. 58, queueing for the 'Last Night'), (Robert Hill, p. 58,
modern 'Last Night'); Broadford Primary School (pp. 40 & 41, both
pictures); Mrs E. Buckley (p. 71, old-fashioned wedding); Burrell
Collection Glasgow Museums (p. 61, all pictures); Camera Press (p. 10,
Patricia Hewitt), (p. 10, Margaret Hodge), (P. Williams, p. 2, The
Trooping of the Colour), (p. 3, Prince Charles at Investiture), (Steward
Mark, p. 37), (K. Goff, p. 5, Prince Charles and Princess Diana); Cumbria
Tourist Board (p. 19, canoeing), (p. 20); Department of Employment,
Crown Copyright (p. 46, factory); The Duke of Edinburgh's Award (p. 2);
Express Newspapers (p. 79, white wedding); Jenny Goodall/Solo (p. 59);
Guardian (Denis Thorpe, p. 73); Helen and Steve Halliwell (p. 71,
modern wedding); Robert Harding Picture Library (Andy Williams, p.
19, angling), (p. 49, woman photographer), (p. 69, terraced houses);
Holmer Green Upper School, Bucks (p. 42) The Hulton Picture Library
(p. 58, Henry Wood conducting); Hulton Deutsch Collection (p. 50,
1920's cabinet maker); The Hutchison Library (Joan Klatchko, p. 7),
(Tony Souter, p. 12, rubbish, p. 19, riding); Impact Photos (Alain le
Garsmeur, p. 14), (Piers Cavendish, p. 42, Eton school boys), (Mohamed
Ansar, p. 80, ethnic mix crowd), (p. 23, man at computer), (Homer Sykes
p. 46, Job Centre); The Independent (p. 37), (p. 30, Suzi Stembridge),
(Nicholas Turpin, p. 30, Roy Clementson), (Craig Easton, p. 53, bill
board), (Nicholas Turpin, p. 77, dancing); Oscar Marzaroli Collection (p.
62); Network (Mike Goldwater, p. 66); John H. Paul (p. 77, nativity play);
Reckitt and Colman Products (p. 53, 'Windolene' woman); Rex Features
(p. 9), (Wil Blanche, p. 19, painting), (p. 69, detached house), (Nils
Jorgensen, p. 82, Trevor MacDonald); Solo (p. 79, Moslem wedding); Frank Spooner Pictures (p.
11, Mary Kaldor), (p. 23, firemen), (R. Tomkins, p. 3, Princess Ann);
Struthers Advertising (p. 60); Elizabeth Whiting & Associates (p. 64)